Dear Oliver

ALSO BY SUSAN R. BARRY

*Fixing My Gaze: A Scientist's Journey Into
Seeing in Three Dimensions*

*Coming to Our Senses: A Boy Who Learned to
See, A Girl Who Learned to Hear, and How We
All Discover the World*

an
UNEXPECTED
FRIENDSHIP
with
OLIVER SACKS

SUSAN R. BARRY

THE EXPERIMENT
NEW YORK

The Experiment, LLC
220 East 23rd Street, Suite 600
New York, NY 10010-4658
theexperimentpublishing.com

THE EXPERIMENT and its colophon are registered trademarks of
The Experiment, LLC. Many of the designations used by manufacturers
and sellers to distinguish their products are claimed as trademarks. Where
those designations appear in this book and The Experiment was aware of a
trademark claim, the designations have been capitalized.

The Experiment's books are available at special discounts when purchased
in bulk for premiums and sales promotions as well as for fundraising or
educational use. For details, contact us at info@theexperimentpublishing.com.

Library of Congress Cataloging-in-Publication Data available upon request

ISBN 978-1-891011-30-6
Ebook ISBN 978-1-891011-31-3

Jacket and text design, and cover illustration, by Beth Bugler
Author photograph by Rosalie Winard

Manufactured in the United States of America

First printing January 2024
10 9 8 7 6 5 4 3 2 1

For Dan,
who encouraged me to send that first letter

Contents

A Haunting Question

OLIVER SACKS, M.D.

2 HORATIO ST. #3G · NEW YORK, NY · 10014
TEL: 212.633.8373 · FAX: 212.633.8928
MAIL@OLIVERSACKS.COM

2/22/07

Dear Sue,
    . . .

        Thanks again for your astounding fist letter.. which was so
rich, and so vivid, in so many ways... You are really a great
letter-writer ---- this, indeed, is how we became truly acquainted...
and this bodes very well for your book. Most of my books have
started as letters to colleagues or friends... then and I think
of nthe book as a ' letter ' to everybody (at least, to anybody
who might be intereste-d). So, for me, the epistolary is an
essential element of writing and communicating... and I suspect that
this
it may also be so with you.

By the time Oliver Sacks wrote these words to me, we had been exchanging letters for more than two years. These were physical letters, written on paper, sealed into envelopes, and sent through the US Postal Service. I was in my fifties and Oliver in his seventies when we began to write. I was a neurobiology professor at Mount Holyoke College while he was a neurologist and bestselling author, well known for his collection of neurological case histories. With each stop at the mailbox, our late-in-life friendship grew. Together, we wrote over 150 letters; the last were exchanged three weeks before Oliver died.

———

We all reach important crossroads in life. Some are obvious, such as when we choose between jobs or places to live. Others are detours that seem minor at the time but turn out to be life-changing. When I sent my "astounding first letter" to Dr. Sacks, I had no idea of the enduring impact it would have on my thinking, my work, and even my identity.

Yet, I almost did not send that letter.

The letter started out as an entry in my "vision diary." Up until age forty-eight, I had been cross-eyed and stereoblind. Most people aim their two eyes at the same location in space so that the information from each is combined in the brain into one three-dimensional image. But my eyes did not point in the same direction. Instead, I looked with one eye and suppressed the information from the other. As a result, I did not see in 3D. Without stereovision, the world appeared cluttered and compressed. But after several months of vision therapy as an adult, I learned to coordinate my eyes and see in stereo depth. The change was revelatory, and I kept a journal in order to record the remarkable changes in my vision. Finally, I had the idea to flesh out my vision story in my diary in the form of a letter to Oliver Sacks.

I knew Dr. Sacks first from his books and admired the way he wrote about his patients with such insight and empathy. But also, I had met him in person. About nine years earlier, my husband, Dan, who was an astronaut, talked with Dr. Sacks when he visited the Johnson Space Center. We then invited him to a reception before Dan's first space shuttle launch, and I was thrilled when he accepted. At the reception, we talked for all of five minutes, but Dr. Sacks asked me a question that haunted me from that time forward. As I went through vision therapy and experienced one visual epiphany after another, I grew increasingly confident of my answer to that question and held many conversations with him in my head. The diary entry was an extension of this inner dialogue. It began with his question:

Dear Dr. Sacks,

We met on January 10, 1996, on the eve of my husband's, Dan Barry's, first space flight on shuttle mission, STS-72. We met at Florida's Space Camp where I hosted a party for my launch guests. During our conversation we talked about the different ways that people perceive the world. I mentioned that my perception of the world was a bit different than most because I saw with only one eye at any one time. I was strabismic,[*] and my view of the world was purely monocular. You asked me if I could imagine what the world would look like when viewed with two eyes. I told you that I thought I could. After all, I am a neurobiology professor at Mount Holyoke College. I have read plenty of papers on visual processing, binocular vision, and stereopsis. I thought that this knowledge gave me some special insight into what I was missing. But, I was wrong.

Over the last two years, thanks to the advice of an exceptional optometrist, a new pair of glasses, and daily vision

---

[*] Strabismus refers to misaligned eyes. Horizontal misalignment leads to crossed eyes (esotropia) or wall eyes (exotropia). In addition, eyes can be vertically misaligned.

therapy, I have learned to use my two eyes together. The change in my vision has been extraordinary. The world is rounder, wider, deeper, more textured, and more detailed. What surprises me most is that I can now see empty space, the space between objects. My vision continues to change and to bring me new delights and surprises each day. I do not know of anyone else who has described such a transformation in their vision, so here is my story in more detail.

What burst out of me then was my vision history, covering nine single-spaced pages. I described how my parents noticed my crossed eyes in the first months after my birth, but the doctors told them I would probably outgrow the condition. When I was two and still cross-eyed, we moved to Connecticut, where I was seen by the prominent eye surgeon Rocko Fasanella at Yale New Haven Hospital. He prescribed glasses and performed three eye-muscle surgeries when I was two, three, and seven years old. After the operations, my eyes looked straighter, though I initially struggled with reading in school and had a hard time learning to ride a bike. I left his care a few years later.

When I was in the fourth grade, I saw Dr. Fasanella for the last time. He removed my glasses and told me that I could now do anything a person with normal vision could do except fly an airplane. No one mentioned to me that I lacked binocular vision,[*] and I remained happily ignorant of the fact until I was a junior in college. I no longer looked cross-eyed and no longer wore thick glasses. I could now enjoy recess without having to wear a cumbersome glasses guard, a contraption that looked like a catcher's mask and took the fun out of dodge ball.[†] As far as I was concerned, I was cured.

---

[*] Binocular vision refers to the ability to simultaneously combine the information from both eyes.

[†] In the 1960s, glasses were actually made of glass, which would have shattered if a ball had hit them, thus the need for the horrible glasses guards.

The surgery was a success cosmetically. My eyes now looked straight. Only my parents noticed when my eyes crossed, at which point, they would issue the command, "Stop wandering." . . . If I wanted to look in the distance, I had to work at diverging my eyes by holding my eyes upward and outward. This effort, combined with the fact that I had large eyes in a small face, gave me the appearance of a startled bug. The kids at school nicknamed me "Frog Eyes." The nickname was not very nice, but I did not care. I was very proud of my straight eyes.

Several years later, I discovered that I had not been "cured." While taking a neurophysiology course in college, I learned that I didn't see the way most people did:

The professor described the development of the visual cortex, ocular dominance columns, monocular and binocular vision, and experiments done on kittens reared with artificial strabismus. He mentioned that these cats probably lacked binocular vision and stereopsis.* I was completely floored. I had no idea that there was a way of seeing the world that I lacked. Perhaps, this explained why I drove poorly and could not operate a sewing machine. I went to the library and struggled through the scientific papers. I tried every stereovision test that I could find and flunked them all. I even learned that one was supposed to see a three-dimensional image through the toy stereoviewer that I had been given after my third operation. I found the old toy in my parents' home but could not see a three-dimensional image with it. Everyone else who tried the toy could.

---

* Stereopsis, or stereovision, allows us to see in 3D and requires simultaneous input from the two eyes. Since the two eyes see from a slightly different angle, they send a slightly different image to the brain. The difference is integrated in the brain, resulting in a single image seen in 3D.

More than twenty years passed, but when I reached midlife, my vision grew more troublesome. When I looked in the distance, everything appeared to jitter. So I found an optometrist, Dr. Theresa Ruggiero, located in a neighboring town, who provided vision therapy for people of all ages. At my first visit, Dr. Ruggiero noted that my eyes were misaligned both horizontally and vertically. My right eye saw lower than my left, so she prescribed a prism for my right eyeglass lens, which reduced the vertical (but not horizontal) disparity between the two eyes. Once I had received the prism glasses, I began vision therapy and was particularly impressed with an eye-alignment exercise called the Brock string, which I described as the "bead exercise."

> Now, here's the amazing part. After the first therapy session with the bead exercise, I went back to my car and happened to glance at the steering wheel. It had "popped out" from the dashboard! I closed one eye, then the other, then looked with both eyes again, and the steering wheel looked different. I decided that the light from the setting sun was playing tricks on me and drove home. But the next day I got up, did the eye exercises (which I continue to do every morning), and got into the car to drive to work. When I looked at the rearview mirror, it had popped out from the windshield.
>
> Over the next several months, my vision was completely transformed. I had no idea what I had been missing. Ordinary things looked extraordinary. Light fixtures floated and water faucets stuck way out into space.

In my letter I added all sorts of everyday yet surprising sights that I had recorded in my diary: how an open door now seemed to stick way out toward me, how the fork held over a bowl of rice looked different because I could see how it was poised in the air above the bowl; how I could see the empty, yet palpable, volumes of space between leaves on trees; how the skull on a horse's skeleton appeared to stick out so far into space that when I first approached it, I actually cried out and jumped back; and how roads appeared to stretch out farther in the horizontal plane, lanes appeared wider, and turns in the car seemed less abrupt.

Everything is sharper. Borders are crisp and distinct, not blurry as previously. Is this due to the prism in the glasses? Is it due to looking at the world with two eyes at the same time? When I use only one eye, I am only getting half the visual information at any one moment. Have I always had binocular cells in my visual cortex? Have they just been waiting for the right input? I don't know all the explanations but I do know that this is absolutely delightful. I experience moments of joy, a childlike glee, like I haven't felt in years. I'm seeing the world in a whole new way.

. . .

Moreover, flat, two-dimensional views also take on more depth. A painting done in perspective appears more three-dimensional than it did in the past. These experiences make me wonder whether a binocular individual can really experience a monocular view of the world simply by closing one eye. Even with one eye closed, that individual can use a lifetime of visual experiences to create a three-dimensional image. I tried to explain to friends my changing view of the world, but they all looked at me uncomfortably. There was no way I could really have them experience the change in my vision. While many people, such as neuroscientists, are aware of the fact that their vision is a creation and interpretation of their brain, they are not reminded of this fact on a glance-by-glance basis as I am. I find that it is best to enjoy quietly and privately my new view of the world.

I told Dr. Sacks about only one incident where my binocular vision has been detrimental. About a year after my vision began to transform, my family went on a trip to Hawaii. While in Kauai, we stopped at a scenic viewing spot overlooking a beautiful canyon. I went right up to the protective railing to take in the view. I felt like I was floating high above an incredibly deep canyon, and the feeling was too strong. I backed away from the railing and took in the view from a distance. Later on that day, while hiking, I felt panicked every time my children or husband moved close to the cliff's edge.

Indeed, I wrote, my new views could sometimes make me feel like I was in a fun house or high on drugs, but mostly I felt comfortable in this new world. And I was extremely grateful.

Imagine a person who saw only in shades of gray suddenly able to see in full color. Such a person would probably be overwhelmed by the beauty of the world. Could they stop looking? Each day, I spend time looking head-on at objects—flowers, my fingers, faucets, anything—in order to get that strong three-dimensional sense. I lie in bed at night looking through stereoviewers. After almost three years, my new vision continues to surprise and delight me. One winter day, I was racing from the classroom to the deli for a quick lunch. After taking only a few steps from the classroom building, I stopped short. The snow was falling lazily around me in large, wet flakes. I could see the space between each flake, and all the flakes together produced a beautiful three-dimensional dance. In the past, the snow would have appeared to fall in a flat sheet in one plane slightly in front of me. I would have felt like I was looking in on the snowfall. But, now, I felt myself within the snowfall, among the snowflakes. Lunch forgotten, I watched the snow fall for several minutes, and, as I watched, I was overcome with a deep sense of joy. A snowfall can be quite beautiful—especially when you see it for the first time.

Once I completed this story and added it to my diary, I felt a sense of peace. By documenting my childhood experiences and combining these with recent journal entries, I had assembled my vision history and thus preserved it. What I was to discover, however, was that this diary entry was not the coda to my visual adventures but rather a prelude to a whole new direction in life. The next day I showed the diary entry to Dan, who encouraged me to send it to Dr. Sacks. I was not so sure. I didn't think anyone would believe me. My acquisition of stereovision at age forty-eight after a lifetime of being cross-eyed challenged a half century of research on "critical periods" in visual development. These studies indicated that stereovision could develop only in early childhood. Since I was a professor of biology and neuroscience at Mount Holyoke College, I was very familiar with this research and had lectured many times on critical periods in class. Indeed, it had taken me many months to convince myself that I was now seeing in 3D. How was I going to convince anyone else? And even if Dr. Sacks believed me, would he appreciate just how novel and wonderful the change in my vision had been? My newfound and hard-earned stereovision meant everything to me. I couldn't stand the idea of someone dismissing my experiences as exaggerated, overly dramatic, and perhaps even delusional. Could I risk sending the letter to Oliver Sacks?

I thought back to my first impressions of Dr. Sacks when I read his book *Awakenings*. In it, he described people frozen for decades in both their movements and thoughts with a severe form of parkinsonism. When he gave them the drug L-dopa, they came alive—moving, speaking, with thoughts crowding into their heads. Dr. Sacks not only observed and listened to these patients but also, most important, tried to imagine what "it *feels* like to have Parkinsonism, to receive L-DOPA, and to be totally transformed." He not only felt *for* his patients but *with* them. My visual transformation was certainly less dramatic than those of his patients but was nevertheless unexpected and life-changing. Perhaps he could imagine how different the world now appeared and felt to me. Hesitant but hopeful, and with Dan's encouragement, I decided that I would send my diary entry to him. I added a brief closing paragraph and my signature.

> That is my story. If you have the time and inclination, I would greatly appreciate your thoughts. And, of course, I eagerly await your next book.
>
> Sincerely yours,
>
> *Sue Barry*

Then, before I lost my nerve, I placed the letter in the mail.

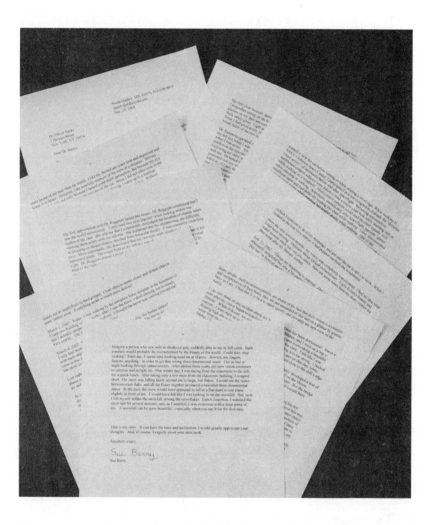

Oliver Comes to Town

Only a few days after receiving my letter, Dr. Sacks responded with one of his own. It arrived in my mailbox so quickly after my first post that I assumed the reply must be a form letter written by an efficient assistant thanking me for my missive but reminding me that Dr. Sacks was a busy man with a large correspondence. Instead, what I received was what I later came to know as vintage Sacks: a letter typed (on a typewriter) on his creamy, thick stationery with a picture of a cuttlefish by his return address. Words were added or crossed out in ink. This letter (like all his future correspondence) was a very personal and attentive response to my descriptions.

I had hoped Dr. Sacks would be interested in my letter from a neurological point of view, but I did not know, at the time of my writing, that he also loved all things stereo and was a proud, "card carrying" member of the New York Stereoscopic Society. Many years later, one of Oliver's close friends described to me how excited he had been to receive my correspondence, and Oliver later told me that my letter made "his hair stand on end." He had always suspected that stereovision provided a qualitatively different and considerably richer worldview than that seen with only one eye, a difference that was not generally appreciated, even by vision scientists. His feelings are clear from the rich and effusive language he used in his reply to me:

OLIVER SACKS, M.D.

2 HORATIO ST. #3G · NEW YORK, NY · 10014
TEL: 212.633.8373 · FAX: 212.633.8928
MAIL@OLIVERSACKS.COM

1)

January 3, 05

Dear Mrs. Barry,

the eve of STS-72 .

I have vivid memories of that night, and Mave received
Christmas/New Year cards from the two of you (or all of you)
over the years, a~~nd~~ *but* have not, I'm afraid, been anything of a
correspondent.

But your letter of the 29th. fills me with amazement ---
and admiration , at your welcoming your ' new ' world ' of *visual*
space and with such openness and wonder - even if it meant
your developing a fear of heights in Kauai - and at your
describing it with such care, and lyricism and accuracy .

Amazement, because it has been ' accepted ' for
years (but clearly Dr. Ruggiero had evidence and thoughts
to the contrary) that if binocular vision was not achieved
by a ' critical age ' (supposedly of some months), then
stereopsis would never occur. Talking to Jerry Bruner, the
psychologist, who was born with congenital cataracts which were
not operated on until he was ~~several~~ *eighteen* months old, seemed to
confirm this. On one occasion he told me how, lacking natural
lenses, with their slight yellowish tint, he could see some way
into what I would call the ' ultraviolet '. I asked him, breathlessly,
what this was like. He answered " I can no more tell you than
you could tell me what stereopsis is like ". Bertrand Russell
contrasts ' knowledge by description ' *and* 'knowledge by acquaintance'
- and you give wonderful descriptions of how utterly they differ,
of how the greatest formal or secondary knowledge can never approach
actual experience... .

I need to thi nk carefully about what you describe, and perhaps
discuss it, if I may, with a friend in visu al physiology. I think
your experience & account ought to be published , ine some form or

OLIVER SACKS, M.D.

2 HORATIO ST. #3G · NEW YORK, NY · 10014
TEL: 212.633.8373 · FAX: 212.633.8928
MAIL@OLIVERSACKS.COM

2)

another, in view of the physiological or psychophysiological
revision it seems to call for ; and, at a more personal level,
the hope it may give for those who have long ' accepted ', at
one level or another, that they are condemned to live in a
' flat ' world.   I also think that the sheer exuberance
you convey, at a sort of visual re-birth, is the sort of
thing which can remind us that stereospsis (like all our
perceptual powers) is a miracle and privilege, and not to
be taken for granted.   ˉˉIf one has (say) stereopsis all
the while, one may indeed take it for granted ; but if,
as with you, one lacked it, and was then ' given ' it -
then it come as a wonder and revelation. This too needs
to be brought out.

     For one reason or another, I have never taken my own
steropsis for granted, but have found it an acute   or
recurrent source of pleasure/ wonder for much of my life.
This led me, as a boy, to experiment with stereo-hotography,
hyper-stereoscopes. pseudo-scopes, etc   (I am still, in
my eighth decade, a member of the New York and also the
International Stereoscopic Society). And it caused me to
pay special attention to an odd experience, in 1974, when
(due to visual restriction, or rather spatial restriction)
I was to discover how my own stereoscopy had been ' collapsed ',
and how it re-expanded   over the course of an hour or so, when
I was replaced in a large space (I enclose a copy of the
relevant pages from A LEG TO STAND ON).

     So, many thanks for writing to me at such length, letting
me share and ponder your experiences ... and let us keep in
touch.

                                                    ⟶

OLIVER SACKS, M.D.
2 HORATIO ST. #3G · NEW YORK, NY · 10014
TEL: 212.633.8373 · FAX: 212.633.8928
MAIL@OLIVERSACKS.COM

3)

Jan 4.   I have taken the liberty of discussing what you describe
            with two colleagues of mine   (Bob Wasserman, an
ophthalmologist, and Ralph Siegel, who works in visual physiology), and
they were as intrigued as I was, and raised a number of questions.
One such , raised by Dr. Wasserman, and related to your mentioning
that your eyes converged a few inches from your face, was whether
you were readily able to thread a needle - which he thinks would
be very difficult without stereopsis.   Dr. Wasserman spoke very
highly of Dr Fasenella.   Another question was whether the vertical
misalignment, which Dr. Ruggiero picked up (and corrected, with a
prism) had been present from the start, or whether it developed
later in your life.   And whether there is still what Dr. Wasserman
calls some ' micro-strabismus ', even though this might not be
symptomatic. Other questions relate to problems with motion-perception
(at least perceiving when you are in motion)

       As you perhaps know I have written about people who have
no perception or idea of color, and would sometimes ask them how
they conceived of color, and whether (if it were possible to
' give ' them the capacity to see it) what this might mean to them.
The question is a tantalizing one, because there is no known way
og ' giving ' an achromatope color ' and, additionally, some of them
say that they think the sudden addition of color - which never
having been perceived before, and so having no associations or ' meaning ' -
might be very confusing to them.   But it is clear that the addition of
' depth ' or ' space ' to your visual world has been (almost) wholly
positive

       S o many qyestions ! Since you have favored me with your
story, and ask my thoughts, I think (over and anove anything I can say
here) that I would like to visit_ you, and perhaps to do so in company
with my old friends & colleagues Bob W and Ralph S, who could explore and
check aspects of your visual perception which I myself could not do. (the
three of us formed a ' team ' when seeing the colorblind painter whom I
wrote it, and the middle-aged man, 'Virgil ' who was given vision after
being virtually blind from birth   I wrote about both of these
in my Anthropologist on Mars book).

You asked for my response to your story, and perhaps this is
too much of a response ! (I am reminded of how, as soon as
I heard Virgil's ' story '. I wanted to flv down to Atlanta
to see him...).

 But give me your thoghts on whether such a visit,
to meet you, and to explore various aspects of visual perception
with you, would be agreeable...

 If it would be, we can work details later.

 Again, thank you so much for sharing your experiences
and thoughts with me, and - really --- opening a new realm.

 My warmest good wishes to you, Dan,

Holy moly! Dr. Sacks wanted to come visit me! I had hoped that he
would reply to my letter with an encouraging, thoughtful note, but,
as he mentioned in his letter, his was indeed a strong response. It's no
wonder, too, that he had his doubts; after all, my acquisition of stereovision in midlife was considered impossible. He needed to check out
my story with the help of his friends, an ophthalmologist and vision

scientist. Either I had an important story to tell or I was delusional. (Either possibility might have been of interest to Dr. Sacks.) I composed a reply right away.

South Hadley, MA 01075
Jan. 8, 2005

Dr. Oliver Sacks
2 Horatio Street, #3G
New York, NY 10014

Dear Dr. Sacks,

Thanks so much for answering my letter so promptly. I would really welcome a visit from you and your colleagues. I very much want my story to be told for all the reasons that you mentioned but especially if my story can help others achieve better binocular vision and a whole new view of the world. My own experience leads me to believe that the adult brain is more plastic than is traditionally thought.

I described to Dr. Sacks how I threaded a needle—by closing my left eye and using only my right. I turned the needle so that its eye faced me and appeared as wide as possible and then directed the thread into the center of the eye. But I also added,

All this aside, I rarely thread a needle because I really dislike sewing and avoid it as much as possible. When I was in eighth grade, like all girls of my generation, I had to take a sewing class at school. Sewing by hand was hard. My stitches were too big, and my eyes fatigued rapidly. Moreover, I never got the hang of the electric sewing machine. I could never get it to sew a straight seam. This was worrisome because I had to sew up a simple dress to complete the class. Worse than that, I had to wear my new dress in front of all the other students during a mock fashion show on the last day of class. Sensing my distress, my parents, always attentive to the needs of their children, actually went out and bought an electric sewing machine. My mother did not know how to use it, and her mother still sewed on a manual machine, which worked with a foot pedal. It was left to my father to show me how to use the new sewing machine. My father did not know how to sew either, but he is an artist and extremely adept with his hands. To my enormous relief, my father quickly mastered the use of the sewing machine and basically made my dress. I graduated from the sewing class and never touched a sewing machine again, but my father really enjoyed the experience! He bought another dress pattern and sewed my mother a dress. Then, for the next fifteen years, he made almost all of my mother's clothes, from bathing suits to winter coats. He even made my wedding dress. So something good did come out of my incompetence with a sewing needle!

I answered some technical questions that Dr. Sacks asked and added that Dr. Ruggiero would be happy to talk with him and share test records taken before and after my vision transformed. "Thank you," I added in closing, "for listening to what I have written."

Shortly after I mailed my letter, Dr. Sacks and I spoke by phone, and we agreed that he would drive up from New York City to my home in Massachusetts on February 9, 2005. I treated his upcoming visit as a serious project by rereading all his books, even researching what I should prepare for lunch. This turned out to be easy. Dr. Sacks had written that bananas and smoked salmon were among his favorite foods so that's what I served him along with homemade minestrone soup, cold cuts, fruit salad, tea, and cookies. I bought the bananas a few days ahead of time because he liked bananas at "the brown, almost liquid stage." On the days leading up to his visit,

I constantly checked the weather, worrying that a snowstorm would prevent his travel. I prepared all the food in advance and set the table the night before.

=====

Oliver Sacks arrived at 11:30 AM on the appointed day. He came with his two friends, Bob Wasserman and Ralph Siegel, who could help him evaluate my vision. I, on the other hand, was alone in the house with our dog, Windy. My son Andy was at the high school, my daughter Jenny was away in college, and Dan was in Houston, Texas, training at Johnson Space Center. Dr. Sacks seemed hungry after the long drive, so I led him and his friends into the dining room. As we chatted over lunch, my concerns about meeting the esteemed Dr. Sacks melted away.

When I read a book, I usually have a pencil in hand in order to make notes, exclamation points, and other markings in the margins. In this way I carry on a conversation with the author. I loved Sacks's books and had been having a mental conversation with him ever since my vision began to change. Now, I was afraid that talking to Oliver Sacks in the flesh would not be like talking to Oliver Sacks on the page. What would I think if he turned out to be pompous and pretentious? But I need not have worried. Dr. Sacks was shy, hesitant, and curious. At one point, I saw him reach down to tentatively pat our little schnauzer, who was foraging under the dining room table. Oliver (for I had started calling him Oliver at this point) kept telling embarrassing stories about himself. While helping me clear away the lunch dishes, he confessed that he had eaten the blueberries I left in my bowl. (I had been too nervous to attempt to pick them up with a spoon or fork.)

After we cleared away the lunch dishes, the clinical investigation began. Oliver, Bob, and Ralph had brought with them vision-testing equipment, which they set up on my dining room table, and a long vision evaluation followed. I was surprised by some of their tools—while some were clinical test kits, others were simple toys. At one point, they gave me the Farnsworth D-15 Dichotomous Color Blindness Test, which I completed perfectly. We all paused. I'm sure Oliver was thinking about Mr. Isaacson (Mr. I.), the artist whom he had written about years before. Mr. Isaacson was a painter who lost all color vision at age sixty-five.* We were quite a contrast, the colorblind painter and I. Mr. I.'s depth perception was excellent and may even have improved after he lost his color vision, while my color vision was excellent but my depth perception below par.

Mostly, my three visitors kept showing me one 3D picture after another and asking me what I saw. They were red/green anaglyphs that we viewed with red/green lenses. Each anaglyph contained two images, one printed in red and one in green, that were superimposed. The two images were of the same object or landscape but were photographed from the slightly different point of view seen by the two eyes. With one eye behind the red lens and one behind the green, each eye saw a slightly different image that, when combined in the brain, resulted in a single picture in 3D. I saw the images popping out and found them to be fun.

We also looked at a classic stereoscopic image, the Stereo Fly, which is often used in eye doctors' offices to test for stereopsis. The fly's wings stand out in depth, and we measured how far the wings popped out for each of us. They popped out the least for me and the most for Oliver. Ralph showed me a random dot stereogram, a stereo pair in which each member looks like a random collection of dots. Upon fusing the two members of the pair, however, one should see an image floating in depth. Since a random dot stereogram contains

* Dr. Sacks wrote about Mr. Isaacson in his 1995 book *An Anthropologist on Mars: Seven Paradoxical Tales.*

no cues to depth that can be seen with just one eye, seeing the floating image is a sure sign that the viewer sees with stereopsis. I could not "get" this stereogram. But then Oliver gave me a stereoviewer through which I saw a collection of words. Again, there were no monocular cues to the 3D arrangement of the words, yet with careful study, I saw and reported the words in the correct depth order.

Even more tests followed. At one point, while looking at a difficult stereogram, Oliver put in front of my eyes a pair of 3D glasses and a picture of a fish. "Whoa," I said, practically jumping out of my chair, "look at that fish! Look at its mouth! It's really sticking out at me!" Then I stopped, feeling embarrassed. No self-respecting fifty-one-year-old lady should get that excited about a 3D fish. Sheepishly, I looked over at Oliver, and he was looking straight at me with this enormous grin on his face. "I like these things, too," he said quietly.

At that moment, everything gelled. I knew now, not just from reading Sacks's books but from meeting him in person, that he was much more than a hard-nosed investigator who would treat me as an interesting case of two eyes and a brain. Oliver understood how much my new vision meant to me. We shared a special delight in the senses, and this forged for me a deep bond with this wise and gentle man.

Even before I had stereovision, I would have said that I saw the world in three dimensions. This was obvious. I moved through a three-dimensional world, and I could use monocular cues, such as perspective, shading and shadows, and object occlusion (objects in front blocking the view of objects behind), to order things in depth. Yet, gaining stereopsis gave me a qualitatively different sense of space.

When I look at myself in the mirror today, I see my reflection located behind the mirror in the reflected space. But when I was stereoblind, I saw my image on the plane of the mirror. Since I did not perceive the empty space between the glass and my reflection, a dirt spot on the mirror pane looked to be on my person, and I would try to clean it off my clothes. Yet, today, if I look at my reflection in the mirror and briefly close one eye, I still see my image as behind the mirror in the reflected space. My stereoviews have transformed the way I see even with one eye. So, when a person who has always had normal stereovision closes one eye, they may not see the world in the same flattened way as someone who has always been stereoblind. They have a lifetime of past stereo experiences to fill in the missing stereo information. Seeing in stereo gave me a sense of the palpable volumes of space between things. This novelty is what was so astonishing and joyful. I was frustrated that I could not explain these changes to many people, even vision scientists. But Oliver understood this from the start.

After lunch and the vision session, we bundled into Oliver's car (where there were copies of the periodic table hanging out of the seat pockets) and drove to my optometrist Dr. Theresa Ruggiero's office. She was very prepared for our visit and ushered us into an examining room, where she recounted my visual history. We discovered that I could do the Brock string (the bead exercise) better at a close distance than Oliver could! Since Oliver was very curious about all the vision therapy equipment that had helped me to see in 3D, Theresa brought him into a vision therapy room where he put on polarized glasses to view polarized vectograms. With these glasses, some images on the vectograms appeared to float toward him while others receded into the distance. Playfully, Theresa suggested that he turn the glasses upside down. Now the images that had floated forward receded and vice versa. For the rest of the afternoon, Oliver continued to sample all the equipment until his eyes grew tired. Then it was time for dinner at an Italian restaurant, where my son, Andy, joined us. The conversation was lively, with Oliver telling neurological stories and Andy reciting, to Oliver's delight, Tom Lehrer's "The Elements" song. Andy did not eat the blueberries in his dessert either, and Oliver commented that this avoidance of blueberries must be a family trait. (Photos from this day can be seen on insert photos 6 and 7.)

But the mood had changed by the next morning. We met at the college inn where my three visitors spent the night. They seemed out of sorts, as if there was some tension between them. Since Oliver had written often of his love of water, I took them all swimming at the Mount Holyoke pool, quickly sneaking them past the gym reception desk. Oliver and I enthusiastically completed our laps while Bob and Ralph lounged. After the swim, we drove back to the campus inn parking lot, where the three got into their car to leave. I hugged Bob and Ralph good-bye while Oliver, standing a little apart, watched and smiled. From a distance, we may have all looked comfortable with each other, but I could still sense the tension among the three of them. As they drove off, I didn't know what to think.

Obsessed but Not Unique

After Oliver's visit, I waited anxiously for a letter, which he wrote on February 15. His letters were written in a different style than his published books. He underlined some words, used parentheses liberally, and many of the paragraphs were full of dashes and dots such as —'s, ---'s, and . . .'s (all reproduced here as a single long dash). These framed his many thoughts, which tumbled out in a staccato fashion. While reading Oliver's letters, I sometimes felt that I was witnessing him in the act of thinking.

OLIVER SACKS, M.D.
2 HORATIO ST. #3G · NEW YORK, NY · 10014
TEL: 212.633.8373 · FAX: 212.633.8928
MAIL@OLIVERSACKS.COM   2/15/05

Dear Sue,

I am so glad it was possible for the three of us (the 'visual team') to visit you, at almost point-blank notice, and spend so much time with you and Dr. Ruggiero.

Oliver then apologized for his delay in writing, which resulted from various travels, and then got to the heart of his letter:

It seems to me, after talking with you, that you did indeed have stereo-experiences at a young age (albeit brief, occasional and only at very close quarters), and that this served as the anlage* of their subsequent, grand development—tho' this is a development which would not have happened without the prism-spectacles, and—equally important—your own assiduous and continuing exercises. It must be quite a rare achievement—Dr. Ruggiero thought it "unique"—and one which (even given the anlage) would/ could not have occurred without your own intense interest and motivation. So it is not to be thought of as a cure, or even hope, for most monoculars.

I was especially struck by your evident delight in stereoscopy—a delight, as you know, which I share myself. If you did not have this, did not value this, I doubt if you would have persisted in the exercises—and what has so much 'reward' and meaning for you might not have much interest or motivation for another. Everyone in the NY Stereoscopic Society is "turned on" by stereoscopy, but this may not be so for the majority of people. Or else they pay no attention to it, take it for granted. An experience like yours (or, in reverse, Isaacson's) shows what a privilege stereo—(or color—) vision is, and how wrong it is to take it as one's entitlement, or for granted.

I don't think you should force yourself to see random-dot stereograms—after all, they have no relevance (or not much) to real life—but I would be interested in whether, with continuing practice, your sense of depth increases, and your ability to experience stereo—from even smaller disparities (as with the test circles on your "Fly"† or Dr. R's "Reindeer"). I think measurement of the subjective height of the fly's wings, once a month or whatever, could be useful here. I will

---

* Anlage refers to the basis or foundation for subsequent development.
† Stereo Fly

have some other thoughts and suggestions after chatting with Bob and Ralph—but, now, just wanted to thank you, from all of us, and to hope that we can visit you again.

Do give my best wishes to Dan—hopefully may see him too next time.

Oliy

Although I never did find out what the tension was among Oliver, Bob, and Ralph at the end of their visit, this letter may have provided a clue. Were they arguing over the interpretation of my case? Oliver may not have rejected my story, but he was approaching it cautiously. After all, my visual experiences contradicted a half century of scientific wisdom that indicated stereovision could develop only during a "critical period" in early childhood. But I disagreed with his interpretations. I didn't think that my acquisition of stereovision at age forty-eight depended on a few stereo experiences in early childhood that served as an "anlage" for later development. Rather, my visual system, like that of people with normal vision, was organized in a binocular way, despite strabismus since infancy.

Stereovision, or stereopsis, results when we are able to fuse the images from the two eyes into a single image seen in 3D. This fusion may be mediated by a subset of binocular cells, that is, neurons in the visual parts of the brain that receive excitatory input from both eyes. We do not know when binocular cells first develop in the human brain. Are they present at birth or do they develop during a critical period in early infancy? Does strabismus in infancy prevent the development of binocular cells and therefore stereopsis, or does strabismus change the way these cells are used?

Our binocular system allows us to fuse images coming from two eyes only if we aim the two eyes at the same region of space at the same time. Since I crossed my eyes, they were aimed at different locations. If I attended to the input from both eyes at the same time, I'd suffer from double vision. So as an infant, I learned to suppress the information from one or the other eye. As a result, the binocular cells that I may have retained received strong input from one eye and very weak input from the other. In vision therapy, I performed sensible eye-teaming exercises that taught me how to point my two eyes simultaneously at the same place in space. This provided correlated input to my binocular cells. Information from the two eyes could now be combined in my binocular neurons, and I could begin to see in 3D.

So, my initial reaction to Dr. Sacks's letter was disappointment and anger, which I expressed in the letter I sent back to him. In retrospect, I'm surprised by my own bluntness.

Feb. 23, 2005

Dr. Oliver Sacks
2 Horatio Street, #3G
New York, NY 10014

Dear Oliver,

Thanks for your letter of February 15. I am glad that your trip through Western Massachusetts went so well, that you were able to pack so many activities into a few days, and especially that you included South Hadley in your travels.

I have been thinking about your letter. I do not know if my experience in gaining binocular vision would serve as a good model for other monocular viewers, but I find your argument on this point a little too pat for several reasons. Although I probably had some binocular experiences as an infant, my early visual experience was closer to that of other strabismic people than it was to individuals with normal binocular vision. If I maintained some binocular cells in my visual cortex, other strabismic people probably have done so as well. Unfortunately, most ophthalmologists and optometrists believe that a strabismic person has no hope of developing any stereoscopic vision. At least, that is the message that I was given by several doctors.

I have just read an account (see enclosed) by an ophthalmologist who lost vision in one eye at age sixty-eight.[*] He had trouble recognizing objects, avoiding obstacles, and even cutting his own fingernails (!). He actually considered himself disabled. His major conclusion from his experience was that adults should not opt for monovision, i.e., they should not adjust their eyewear so that one eye is used to see far and the other to see near. He never questioned, however, whether attempts should be made to improve binocular vision in strabismic patients, probably because he did not think this was possible.

You wrote that most people do not appreciate stereopsis. That is probably true. An individual may realize the value of stereopsis only when they, like the ophthalmologist I mentioned above, lose it due to some calamity. Most people simply assume that they see the world in three dimensions because the world is in three dimensions (string theory aside). They are unaware that their brain reconstructs a three-dimensional image by interpreting and manipulating information provided by their two-dimensional retinae. Even the great early students of optics, such as Euclid, Newton, and da Vinci, never discovered or described stereopsis.

But I wonder how a stereoblind person would react to stereopsis. Would they appreciate stereovision more than a

---

[*] P. E. Romano, "A case of acute loss of binocular vision and stereoscopic depth perception (The misery of acute monovision, having been binocular for 68 years)," *Binocul Vis Strabismus Q* 18, no. 1 (2003): 51–55.

normal binocular person? Would they be as delighted as I
am? I would not presume to know how others would react
because the only stereoblind person I know who developed
some moderate stereopsis is me. Most stereoblind people,
even if they have functional vision in both eyes, never get
the chance to find out.

I went to see Dr. Ruggiero to improve my day-to-day
vision. I did not think I was capable of stereovision and was
not hoping to attain it, although I was intrigued by Dr.
Ruggiero's comments that the world had popped out for some
of her patients. About ten years before seeing Dr. Ruggiero, I
had seen an ophthalmologist in Holyoke and complained to
him that the world appeared to shimmer at a distance. . . . He
examined my vision in the usual way, by testing the acuity of
each eye separately. He reported to me that the vision in each
eye was correctible to 20/20 and that, therefore, my concerns
were "all in my head." I tried to accept his advice, but an
experience several years later made me realize that I was
increasingly confining my visual exploration of the world to
within ten to twenty feet of my body.

I was co-teaching an eighty-student introductory biology
course with one of my sharp-eyed colleagues. She asked me
why I never acknowledged the students who raised their
hands in the back of the 100-seat lecture hall. I told her that
I was unaware that there were students back there with
questions even though I was wearing my glasses. She then
positioned herself in the classroom behind all the students.
Whenever a hand popped up in the back of the class, she
would wave her arms wildly trying to get my attention. Then
she would gesture in an exaggerated manner in the direction
of the student with the question. The students may have
seen all these crazy antics, but they were too polite to say
anything. It was funny but also frustrating.

Thus, when I went to see Dr. Ruggiero, I was determined to find a way to see more comfortably at a distance, to stabilize my gaze, to drive with more confidence. I was very excited by the improvement in my vision provided by the prism in my eyeglasses. Dr. Ruggiero warned me that vision therapy might not work for me, and that it was hard and tedious. But, thankfully, she gave me the option to try it. I may work harder at vision therapy than others. I like practicing things again and again (i.e., swimming laps). However, my vision began to change as soon as I began the bead exercise. I had almost immediate positive feedback, which kept me working. Moreover, my vision improved not just in terms of depth perception but also in terms of overall clarity. . . . Borders became sharper, and everything appeared more distinct.

If doctors make the assumption that their patients will not be willing to work at vision therapy or that a stereoblind person may not value the emergence of crisper vision and stereopsis, then doctors will never give their patients the chance or the choice to pursue treatment. That choice should be made by the patient, not by the doctor. We are caught in a vicious cycle in which it is assumed that vision therapy will not help strabismic people so that it is not provided often enough to reach any real conclusions. The experiment, simply, has not been tried.

Now that I vented my frustrations on this issue, I will admit that I have a special affection for stereoscopy. I derive great pleasure from the stereo book on ocean life that you gave me. I look at it almost every night and can almost feel myself being sucked into the reef canyons or into the tentacles of a jellyfish. I enjoyed every minute of your visit, even my failed attempts to see images in random dot stereograms, and I like Bob and Ralph very much. You and your friends are welcome to visit any time you like. Dan and

I can also come down to New York as we enjoy our trips to
the big city.

Take care,

Sue

Just as I had been intrigued by Oliver's question at our first
meeting—"Can you imagine what it's like to see with two eyes?"—I
was now obsessed with Oliver's questions posed in his February 15
letter. Was I unique in my acquisition of stereopsis? Would other
stereoblind people be as amazed and overjoyed with stereopsis as I was?
Was my reaction simply over the top? Even though I had mentioned
in my initial letter that I did not know anyone else who had acquired
stereovision in adulthood, I hated being called unique. Since I was
very cross-eyed as a child, I had felt like an oddity. Even after my eyes
were surgically straightened, I had so much trouble learning to read,
ride a bike, and sew that I knew something about me was off. Perhaps
other people with strabismus could learn to see in 3D if given the right
training. I *had* to find people like myself. So I turned to the internet,
and it was not long before I found them. Fifteen days after sending
Dr. Sacks the first angry letter, I sent him another describing other
people who had not only gained stereovision as adults but also reacted
to their new way of seeing with the same exuberance that I did.

March 8, 2005

Dr. Oliver Sacks
2 Horatio Street, #3G
New York, NY 10014

Dear Oliver,

. . .

Below is a quote from a woman named Rachel Cooper who
suffered from lazy eye and monocular vision and acquired

stereopsis at age 33. The change in her vision was so compelling that she founded an organization and website, the Optometrists Network, in order to help others locate vision therapists. Below are quotes from her own story describing the changes in her vision:

. . .

I'll admit that when I first began to see the visual world pop out in 3D I felt a lot like a formerly paralyzed person jumping out of a wheelchair and doing a jig. It felt like a miracle.

Ever since the day I saw the world popping out in 3D for the first time, I've wanted to tell others to appreciate the miracle of normal depth perception and 3D vision. You SEE, if you overcome a disability, you very likely won't take what you've gained for granted. What other people call normal will always be special to you!

P.S. Since I've acquired stereovision people ask me to describe what it was like when I didn't have it. Here is a very short answer. The visual world looked flat. It felt like I was **here** and everything I was looking at was **over there**. I couldn't visually perceive or measure the space between me and other objects. Now that I see in 3D it feels like I am **IN** the world. Empty space looks and feels palpable, tangible— ALIVE!

Well, friends, I've got to sign off for now. Remember . . . life really is better in 3D.

Rachel's statements supported my arguments nicely, so I continued by writing,

I underlined the sentences in the above quote because these words reflect exactly my experience. If you read the P.S. in

Rachel Cooper's writings and my description of watching a snowfall at the end of my first letter to you, they describe exactly the same experience of perceiving space before and after acquiring stereopsis.

Rachel Cooper writes that a stereoblind person will not take stereopsis for granted as a normal binocular viewer might. I agree. Acquiring stereopsis is not the same, for example, as getting an update on your glasses prescription for your nearsighted eyes. When you get a new prescription, you might notice for a day or two that your vision is sharper. But, soon, you come to expect this sharpness of vision and give it no more thought. Updating your glasses prescription is not a life-changing event.

Acquiring stereopsis, even the moderate amount of stereopsis that I possess, is a completely different story. As a biology professor, I have taught the mechanics of stereopsis to countless students over the years. I know, theoretically, what stereopsis is all about. However, I had no experience of stereoscopy. I could <u>not</u> imagine what it was like although I thought I could. The brief moments that I mentioned to you of seeing plants up close in greater depth were too fleeting and too infrequent to make sense of them. One simply cannot imagine how the world looks with stereopsis if one has no experience of it. Thus, the acquisition of stereopsis comes as a huge surprise and gift. Seeing the space between objects is completely novel. Three years and millions of visual impressions later, I am still amazed on a daily basis by my new vision. The acquisition of stereopsis <u>is</u> a life-changing event.

Then I added quotes from two more people who gained stereopsis as adults and closed the letter with the following paragraphs:

For me, it is tremendously exciting to discover other people
who have experienced a visual transformation similar to my
own. However, I am always a bit suspicious of what I read
on the web. I wrote a letter to the Optometrists Network
and sent emails to several optometrists who have discussed
vision therapy on their websites. My hope is that I will
be able to locate and correspond with other individuals
who share my excitement in obtaining stereopsis. If I am
successful, I will pass on their stories to you.

Dan, Andy, and I along with Dan's three gregarious
sisters are heading off to the tropics for a week's vacation.
(Poor Jenny is stuck working in college.) Perhaps, when we
return, spring will be on its way.

Please send my best wishes to Bob and Ralph.

Stereoscopically yours,

Sue

A few days later, thanks to some highly efficient office worker at
Yale New Haven Hospital, my surgical records from my three operations, in 1956, 1957, and 1961, were exhumed from some storage
facility in New Haven and sent to me. I sent those on to Oliver, too.

Oliver wrote back on March 11 with a cautious but supportive
note, also pointing out that he called me "unique" because that is
how I described myself in my original letter! He answered my sign-off
("stereoscopically yours") with one of his own. I assume he wanted to
keep the letter to one page, which is why his sign-off appeared upside
down and toward the top of the page. He must have reinserted the
letter sideways into his typewriter to add the postscript.

OLIVER SACKS, M.D.

2 HORATIO ST. #3G · NEW YORK. NY · 10014
TEL: 212.633.6373 · FAX: 212.633.8928
MAIL@OLIVERSACKS.COM

March 11, 05

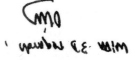

Dear Sue,

       I have just got back from (a week in) London, rather
jet-lagged, and with a huge mass of mail whi ch has accumulated   -
but I am happy to find in it your letter of March 8, and
the old records which wer exhumed (and of which I have sent
a copy to Bob).

       It is going to take me   -   perhaps all of us - a ce rtain
time (and exploring) to gain perspective here. I really
have no idea how common, or otherwise, the achievement of
stereoscopy (in adult life) is   -   nor the pre-requisites
for this (in terms of physiological potential, and in terms
of the techniques and work needed to realize the potential).
If I used the words ' rare ' or ' unique ' it is because
you, in your original letter, said that you knew of no
comparable accounts, and because you r optometrist too
indicated that, in her experience at least, such achievements
of stereoscopy were not common.

       It is intriguing, therefore, that you have been able to
'google ' some accounts seemingly similar to your own
experience - and I understand how exciting this must be
for you ; though I also think you are right to feel
a certain reserve or caution regarding them.   I think that
all such testimonies have to be subjected to careful investigation.
The ' Achromatopsia ' Network - which I mention at the end
of ' The Island of th e Color Blind ' - is a great comfort
(and resource) to people with (retinal) achromatopsia -
and it may be that there is a comparable 'stereopsia ' network -
so I will be very interest in whatever contacts you are able to
make. Meanwhile I shall forward your letter to Bob and Ralph -
as well as the fascinating account of the man who lost stereopsis.

PS When I was in England I spoke of you to Professor Richard Gregory, who is
the world's greatest expert on visual perception in general and stereopsis in
particular. Would that you could go to his Lab in Bristol .

Oliver's letter spurred me to a three-week period of intensive research, of hours reading scientific papers and corresponding with others who had learned to see in 3D and with the optometrists who had helped them. I was consumed by this work, determined to prove to Oliver that I was not unique. To me, he represented all the doubters in the world (most of the scientific and medical establishment), but he was also a deep-thinking, empathetic, and open-minded person. By mid-April I had acquired enough case histories to send Oliver a long missive, more a battle cry than a letter:

April 12, 2005

Dr. Oliver Sacks
2 Horatio Street, #3G
New York, NY 10014

Dear Oliver,

I hope this letter finds you well and happily driving around in that fine hybrid car you like to write about, the car with the laminated copies of the periodic table hanging out of the pockets behind the front seats.

When I got back from vacation three weeks ago, I began a search for individuals who developed stereovision in adult life.

Just as Oliver had suggested in his last letter, I needed to find people like me. What followed was a ten-page, single spaced letter (with an eleventh page of references to scientific papers I had cited). In it, I recounted the experiences of four patients who gained stereopsis as adults, and I included the conversations with five behavioral (also called developmental) optometrists. I quoted from an email exchange with Margaret Livingtone at Harvard, a vision scientist who suspected that I may have always had binocular cells but was just learning how to use them. I delved into the scientific literature, summarizing papers that presented evidence for residual binocular function in experimental animals made strabismic in infancy. And I reminded Oliver that he didn't like being called "unique" either.

> My vision story has some parallels with your own experience described in *A Leg to Stand On*. You wrote that your surgeon refused to acknowledge that there was anything wrong with your leg after surgery even though you had no proprioceptive* input from, internal knowledge of, and voluntary control of the limb. (I was amused to read that you did not like being called "unique" either when you complained to the medical staff about the unorthodox condition of your leg.) After surgery your leg was fixed anatomically so that the surgery was considered successful even though the leg did not work. Similarly, a very competent eye surgeon straightened my eyes cosmetically, but I had little or no functional binocular vision. We both needed therapy to *relearn* how to walk or how to see.

I pointed out that the vision therapy techniques that Oliver had seen in Dr. Ruggiero's office, such as the Brock string, taught me in manageable, incremental steps how to align my eyes. These procedures were sensible and straightforward and certainly not based on superstition or crackpot ideas.

> As soon as I learned to fixate simultaneously the same point with both eyes, I began to see in depth. As I was able to maintain fixation with both eyes on more distant points, I was able to see objects pop out at more distant locations.

---

* Proprioception is your body's ability to sense your own movements, to know where your limbs are in space without looking at them. Thanks to proprioception, for example, you can touch your finger to your nose with your eyes closed.

In hindsight, the whole process seems surprisingly straightforward. It troubles me that these sensible rehabilitation techniques are not generally available to patients with strabismus, amblyopia,* and other conditions affecting binocular vision.

With this last statement, I touched upon a delicate subject: the deep antagonism between ophthalmologists who treat strabismus with surgery and developmental/behavioral optometrists who treat strabismus with vision therapy. Since the two types of doctors rarely work together, patients do not get the comprehensive treatment they may need.

Ophthalmologists can straighten cosmetically the eyes of a strabismic person, but the surgery does not always lead to a change in vision. It is the vision therapist who teaches the patient <u>how to see</u> with the two eyes together and develop stereovision.

With Oliver's interest in and validation of my experience, I wanted, more than ever, to have my story told. So I closed with this paragraph:

Poor binocular vision and stereoblindness are not great tragedies. Stereoblindness is not nearly as debilitating as being blind, deaf, or afflicted with a severe neurological condition. However, stereoblindness does make day-to-day life more difficult because it makes it harder to master such basic skills as reading and driving. And, stereoblindness robs one of a great deal of the richness and beauty of the visual

---

* Amblyopia is a visual condition in which there is reduction in vision in one or both eyes that cannot be corrected by lenses and is not due to eye disease. Amblyopia is colloquially called "lazy eye."

world. Without the sense of space provided by stereopsis, a stereoblind person is always looking in on the world and does not really feel a part of their three-dimensional surroundings. When a stereoblind person begins to see the world enlarge and objects pop out, they know they have received a great gift. This gift, this capacity for binocular vision and stereopsis, may lie dormant in the brain circuits of many people with strabismus and amblyopia. With the proper therapy, these individuals may revive and reorganize their latent binocular systems and, thus, learn to see the world in more detail, with greater clarity, and in depth.

After such a serious and very long letter to which I appended a reference list of twelve articles from scientific journals, I needed to lighten the mood so I signed off with:

Yours in multiple dimensions,

Sue

If Oliver felt besieged by my barrage of letters, he never let on.* Despite his travels, he answered my April 12 letter right away. And his letter contained some intriguing information.

---

* Recently, I read in Lawrence Weschler's book *And How Are You, Dr. Sacks?* that Oliver wrote an eighty-eight-page letter to the great Soviet psychologist A. R. Luria, so my missives were brief in comparison.

OLIVER SACKS, M.D.

2 HORATIO ST. #3G · NEW YORK, NY · 10014
TEL: 212.633.8373 · FAX: 212.633.8928
MAIL@OLIVERSACKS.COM

April 16, 05

Dear Sue,

    Thank you for your most remarkable letter of the 12th which
I have just read with great attention and fascination (but it will
require several re-readings, I suspect). You have done a huge
amount of research, both in the literature, and in contacting
other individuals, since your last letter - and a huge amount
of thinking : indeed your experience (and that of others),
as the French say, " gives one furiously to think ".

    I am not sure (I have been away a lot) whether I acknowledged
your previous letter, your relaying the early information about
surgery etc, and the fascinating case=history of the doctor
rendered monoular .. but if I did not, let me thank you ,
belatedly, now.   I will, of course, send a copy of your new
(April 12) letter to Bob Wasserman and to Ralph (whom I will
be seeing in a couple of days).

    I was most interested by Margerie Livingstone's letter   - and
when I met Hubel and Wiesel at a recent meeting of the NY Academy
of Sciences (I had met them both before), I spoke to them briefly
about your experiences, and they were both intrigued, and encouraged
me to explore more. There may be a dogma, as you say, but they
themselves are as open as can be ..   I feel, and have felt, since
receiving your first letter, that all these issues need a wide (and
wise) publication, but am not sure at the moment how this would be
best done, and who should do it. with stereoplasm.   Oliv

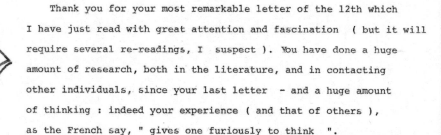

In his letter, Oliver mistyped Margaret Livingstone's first name. The little drawings are Oliver's hand-drawn stereo pairs. One member of the pair approximates the image as seen by the right eye and the other by the left eye. I had fun "free-fusing" the pair into a single image seen in stereo depth. To do this, I either crossed my eyes for convergent fusion or looked beyond the page for divergent fusion.

I ruminated over Oliver's letter for quite some time, especially this sentence: "I feel, and have felt, since receiving your first letter, that all these issues need a wide (and wise) publication, but am not sure at the moment how this would be best done, and who should do it." My guess is that Oliver did not want to steal my story from me. I, on the other hand, did not have the confidence to publish the story on my own. When I was little and cross-eyed, I felt like a freak at times. My difficulties learning to do everyday activities such as reading, bicycling, and driving made me feel inadequate. I would have been crushed if I wrote up my story and was labeled as ignorant, naive, or even delusional. I never spelled all this out to Oliver, but I think he figured it out.

What's more, Oliver's letter contained a very intriguing detail. He had described my case to Drs. Hubel and Wiesel, Nobel laureates and the very scientists who had coined the term "critical period" with regard to visual development. If they were, as Oliver wrote, "as open as can be," then maybe I should pluck up the courage to write to them. So, on May 7, 2005, I sent David Hubel an email. He wrote back on May 27, apologizing for the delay and explaining that he had just recovered from shingles: "Thank you so much for the fascinating letter describing your experience with strabismus, and the dramatic recovery you describe following alignment of your eyes, and the therapy lessons." He felt "with regret," that his and Wiesel's story about strabismus was incomplete. No one knew whether the binocular cells that mediate stereopsis were present in newborn monkeys or people though he predicted that they were. If these cells were present in the newborn, then they may indeed be present in someone—like me—who had strabismus from infancy. "From your description, if I had to guess," Hubel wrote, "I would say that your ability to do stereo may have been present all along, and that the eye alignment was too poor to demonstrate it. Once that got corrected and fusion obtained, the stereopsis became evident." He even suggested (and this proved to be true) that with more training my stereopsis would improve.

Hubel had also received a letter from Oliver and had written to him with the same response. He ended his letter to me by offering to send me his newly published book, *Brain and Visual Perception*. Dr. Hubel had won the Nobel Prize in part for his work on the critical period. My visual changes challenged this very concept, and yet he believed my story. By the time I got to the end of his email, I was trembling.

=====

Twelve days later, on June 8, Oliver gave me a call. He first called our house and spoke to Dan, who told him that I was in Woods Hole, Massachusetts, for the summer, directing the Grass Fellowship program at the Marine Biological Laboratory (MBL). Dan and the kids were to join me there as soon as the kids' school year ended, so he suggested that Oliver come visit us in August when the *Noctiluca*, a bioluminescent microorganism, congregated in the waters around Cape Cod. That got Oliver's attention. The only thing better than swimming was swimming in a bioluminescent sea.

When Oliver reached me by phone at the lab in Woods Hole, we first talked about *Noctiluca* and a possible visit. Then, rather hesitantly, Oliver told me that he had written a story about me and wanted to make sure that was OK. OK? Of course, that was OK. Oliver asked if I thought I was obsessive. I thought back to all the late-night research I had done and to my barrage of letters, all to prove to him that my vision story was not unique. Yes, I told him, I could be obsessive. I didn't mind his question. *It takes one to know one*, I thought.

I suspect that all my letters and research as well as Hubel's thoughts helped convince Oliver to write and publish my story, but there was something more. He considered not only my performance on various vision tests but also the passion with which I reacted to and described my new sights. He was struck by my delight in my new way of seeing and the "lyrical" (as he described it) way I wrote about it. He did not interpret my "obsessiveness" and exuberance as hysterical or delusional. He took me seriously and, in so doing, recognized that I had undergone a profound change in my vision.

And this change in my vision brought on other transformations, changes that surprised me but may not have surprised the more holistic-thinking Oliver. When, in 1976, I first met my husband, an electrical engineer, he described me as a "low-pass filter," a description intended to be complimentary and indicating that I was steady and calm. But I did not feel like that in the least anymore. With each glance, everything I saw took on a new look. I could see the volume and 3D shape of the empty space between things. Tree branches reached out toward me; light fixtures floated. A trip to the produce section of the supermarket, with all its sights and smells, could send me into a sort of ecstasy. All this was very confusing to a hard-core scientist like me, but corresponding with Oliver helped me understand these changes. As I wrote to Oliver, eight years later, on July 9, 2013,

Dear Oliver

. . .

The change in my vision also brought on a crisis. I had
always relied on reductionist science for its explanatory
powers. (Ahh—I've used the word "powers," one of your
favorite words!) But now I had experienced neuroscience
both from the outside and the inside. While I certainly don't
subscribe to Descartes' dualism,* I discovered that we could
explain less with our experiments and diagrams than we
thought. A map of the changing visual circuits in my brain,
no matter how precise, complete, and detailed, could never
explain the global perceptual changes, the epiphanies, and
strong emotions I experienced when I began to see in stereo.

. . .

What's more, scientists and physicians, so wed to the
doctrine of the critical period, had been wrong about my
visual capabilities. (However, David Hubel could not have
been more supportive to me or more generous with his
time.) The mindset of the critical period still prevents people
with strabismus and amblyopia from receiving the therapy
they need. I felt like rejecting all of reductionist science; its
outlook was too narrow, too fragmented (a description
you've used and I like), and far too dehumanizing. How
could I remain a science professor if I was so disillusioned?

I found some answers in your own writings, in particular
your description of your own disillusionment in *A Leg to
Stand On*. In the last chapter, you ranted against the
constricted focus of Jackson, Sherrington, Head, Leont'ev,
Zaporozhets, and even Luria,† but you did not reject them.

---

* Descartes believed that the thinking mind and the physical brain were entirely separate.
† These men were all brilliant neurologists, and A. R. Luria, through his letters to Oliver, was a mentor to him.

They were trapped in the "predicament of science itself." Learn from the mechanisms and schemata they describe but recognize that these parts do not add up to the whole. They do not explain the overall style, spontaneity, perceptions, unity—the gestalt—of a whole individual. Your essay "Scotoma: Forgetting and Neglect in Science"* gave me a more objective and historical way to look at my own experience. I was very lucky to have stumbled upon vision therapy procedures, pioneered by Frederick Brock, a brilliant but largely forgotten optometrist, whose holistic ideas were well ahead of his time (prematurity). Gradually, I realized I needed to read more broadly, to absorb ideas from other disciplines. I didn't need to reject reductionist science; I just needed to take it off its pedestal. Thus, I went from feeling disillusioned to feeling liberated.

What do you do when your own observations contradict common beliefs or entrenched dogma? Do you dismiss your own observations as biased and flawed or do you question authority? By attending so conscientiously to my letters, Oliver gave me the confidence to trust my own observations.

What's more, obsessiveness was not the only trait that Oliver and I shared. We both thought best by writing things down. My letters to Oliver didn't stop after he wrote about me. It was through our continuing correspondence that I examined, organized, and eventually published my own story. I went from patient to agent to author. But I am getting ahead of myself. First came "Stereo Sue."

---

* This essay first appeared in R. B. Silvers, *Hidden Histories of Science* (New York: New York Review of Books, 1995) and later in O. Sacks, *The River of Consciousness* (New York: Alfred A. Knopf, 2017).

Night Lights

66 "I don't mind if you transform me from a person into a character," I wrote in my next letter to Oliver (June 13, 2005), paraphrasing a quote from Primo Levi that Oliver had included in his
acknowledgments to his memoir of his childhood, *Uncle Tungsten*.
It was my way of telling Oliver that I trusted him to write my story
sympathetically and accurately. I also included the whole of my
vision diary and answers to several technical questions that Oliver
had asked during our phone call. I was in Woods Hole at the time,
directing the MBL Grass Fellowship program and returning home
to South Hadley on the weekends. So after answering all of Oliver's
questions regarding my vision, I happily wrote about some of the
many delights that Oliver and I both loved about Woods Hole:

> On a very different note, I spent some time observing the
> squid in one of the holding tanks at MBL the other day. The
> squid's eyes are located laterally in the back of their heads.
> In this position, I bet they can see both in front and behind,
> which makes sense, since they swim both forward and
> backward. I found a paper written by J. Zed Young comparing
> the eye muscles in the octopus and squid. The squid has

extra eye muscles used for eye convergence and presumably binocular vision, which may be very helpful in accurately shooting out their tentacles to capture prey.

I recently read your book *Oaxaca Journal* and enjoyed it very much. I learned a new word, too—fossicker.[*] (I had to look it up.) I've gone on numerous hikes and camping trips with botanists and birders, and they remind me of your pteridologists.[†] I have always been impressed with how much detail and drama a good naturalist sees in the outside world. I remember once bird-watching at the seashore with an ornithologist friend. We heard a peep and he said, before seeing the bird, "Ah, a horned grebe—and in spring plumage." All this from one peep.

This weekend, I went home to South Hadley to see Dan and Andy. By the time I got off the bus on Sunday back in Woods Hole, I felt uncomfortable and restless, so I went straight to the beach for my first ocean swim of the summer. The water was almost cold enough to stop one's circulation, and the only other warm-blooded creature in the ocean with me was one fanatic ball-retrieving dog. Nevertheless, I enjoyed the swim, and it definitely got rid of the feeling that you get from riding on a bus for several hours.

I asked one of my protozooloigist friends today about the *Noctiluca* bloom. She said the *Noctiluca* usually show up in late July and peak in August. She did not know how the red tide, a bloom of *Alexandrium fundyense*, would affect the *Noctiluca* population, but she did not think it would have a big effect. You are most welcome to visit in August to swim with the *Noctiluca*.

---

[*] A fossicker is someone who searches for precious stones and fossils.
[†] A pteridologist is a person who studies ferns.

Please let me know if you need any other information. I have also included my email exchange with David Hubel and your very own Brock string as an exercise for your vision.

Binocularly yours,

Sue

Oliver wrote back five days later.

OLIVER SACKS, M.D.
2 HORATIO ST. #3G · NEW YORK, NY · 10014
TEL: 212.633.8373 · FAX: 212.633.8928
MAIL@OLIVERSACKS.COM

June 18/19? 05
(not sure, jet-lagged, disoriented!)

Dear Sue,

A very brief letter because I have just come back from a whirlwind visit to Alaska.

Oliver outlined his recent travels and added that he was about to go to London. Then in a paragraph, replete with adjectives, he turned to the main subject of his letter, my vision story:

Thank you for you extremely detailed, invaluable account clarifying the "stages" of stereopsis, and your extraordinary diary, including the crucial leading-up days in the third week of February '02[*]—and thank you too for being amenable to my writing about you and your experiences, in the context of stereopsis-in-general. I promise I will respect them.

Oliver was still revising the story and would send it to me when he returned from his travels. He closed by writing,

---

[*] When Oliver wrote about "the third week in February," he was referring to the time when I first saw in 3D.

I got a charming note from Roger Hanlon,* and hope I can come up (with Bob, also an avid wind-surfer, kayaker etc) to Woods Hole in July, see you both/all, and enjoy the then luminescent hydrodynamics of swimming in the sea.

The sign-off reads "With all my thanks again, and best wishes, Oliver."

"Dear Globetrotter," I wrote in my June 27 letter to Oliver, advising him that August would be the best time to swim with the bioluminescent *Noctiluca*. Oliver's birthday was July 9, so I sent him a trivet with a picture of a squid. His next letter was handwritten and contained one of Oliver's many made-up words and a reference to his unusual association with the chemical elements. I've provided a transcription of the letter below.

* Roger Hanlon is a senior scientist at the Marine Biological Laboratory who has traveled the world studying cephalopods. These animals, including octopus, squid, and cuttlefish, are among Oliver's favorite creatures. Roger's stunning photographs and original observations of cephalopods can be found in his two beautifully illustrated scientific books, *Cephalopod Behavior* and *Octopus, Squid & Cuttlefish*, as well as on his TED talk and on other videos online.

OLIVER SACKS, M.D.
2 HORATIO ST. #3G · NEW YORK, NY · 10014
TEL: 212.633.8373 · FAX: 212.633.8928
MAIL@OLIVERSACKS.COM

July 15/05

Dear Sue,

Thank you so much for your nice
birthday card, and the handsome squid
teiver (which I have added to my
teuthobilia). It is hafnium now, as you
say, and I have ordered myself a
little oblivion ingot of it as a lest I
forget ...

    · · ·

I hope I can stay over with you
and/or Roger ~~because~~ when I am in
Wood's Hole, and swim, kayak, feast —
and talk about robots, space, invertebrates
and — I concur! stereopsis.

    · · ·

My best to you both,

Oliver

July 15/05

Dear Sue,

Thank you so much for your nice birthday card, and
the handsome squid trivet (which I have added to my
teuthobilia*). It is hafnium now, as you say, and I have
ordered myself a little, bluish ingot of this lest I forget.†

. . .

I hope I can stay over with you and/or Roger when I am
in Woods Hole, and swim, kayak, feast—and talk about
robots, space, invertebrates and—of course! stereopsis.

. . .

My best to you both,

Oliver

On July 28, I received an email from Kate Edgar, Oliver's longtime editor and personal assistant:

I just sent a FedEx to you at MBL with a draft of Oliver's
piece, currently called "Stereo Sue." It should reach you
tomorrow mid-day. We will eagerly await your feedback!

The article arrived by FedEx the next day, and I was delighted
with what I read. Oliver had captured my astonishment and joy
at first seeing in 3D and the novelty of this experience. He wrote,
"But one cannot convey to the stereo-blind what stereopsis is *like*;

---

* Teuthis is a genus of squid. Oliver made up the word "teuthobilia."

† Oliver equated people's ages with the atomic numbers of the elements. He had just turned
seventy-two, the atomic number of hafnium.

the subjective quality, the quale,* of stereopsis is unique and no less remarkable than that of color."

Four days later, I sent an email back to Kate with my comments, mostly changes that should be made for accuracy, though I did argue with Oliver about the concept of the critical period. Later that day, Oliver responded with an email (via Kate; Oliver didn't use computers) thanking me for my prompt and careful reading of the manuscript. He had made most of the changes I suggested.

Oliver and Bob arrived in Woods Hole on August 11, 2005, and stayed two nights with Roger Hanlon and two nights with us. When preparing Oliver's bedroom, I left a toy View-Master by his night table, since he, like me, enjoyed looking at these stereo pictures when first getting into bed. The first thing Oliver did upon entering our house was to give me a hug and a manila folder containing a newly revised version of "Stereo Sue" as well as copies of letters from several scientists he had consulted.

The next morning, I found Oliver up early. He had spread all his papers on the dining room table and, fountain pen in hand, was working hard. I mentioned that *Awakenings* was the first of his books that I had read. Since my mother had Parkinson's disease, I was tremendously moved by the stories in this book and became hooked on his writing. Oliver told me that if I read carefully, I could probably find the point in the book where, after injuring his shoulder, he had to dictate rather than write down the words.

Not surprisingly, we spent most of our time together swimming. I took Oliver and Bob on my favorite swim from Stony Beach to a stone pier at Penzance Point. Oliver started out with such a strong, steady stroke that it took him far out to sea. Alarmed, Bob and I called him in

* In their book, *Phantoms in the Brain*, V. S. Ramachandran and S. Blakeslee define quale (plural: qualia) as "the raw feel of sensations such as the subjective quality of 'pain' or 'red' or 'gnocchi with truffles.'"

closer to shore. When we reached the stone pier, Oliver gazed for quite some time at the seaweed growing there, just as he carefully studied the lichen on the steps leading up to our house. Nothing was too modest or small to escape his attention or sympathy.

On the way home from the beach, I walked back with Bob while Oliver continued slightly ahead. When we reached the front yard of our house, I saw something orange out of the corner of my eye. I turned to look and recognized Oliver's bathing suit hanging to dry on a tree branch. "Oh no!" I panicked. "He took off his bathing suit, and he isn't wearing anything else!" Slowly, I turned to look at Oliver, but he had wrapped his large beach towel securely around his waist, and seeing my alarmed expression, smiled sheepishly.

By a lucky coincidence, we were renting a house across the street from a family whom Oliver had described in his book *Seeing Voices*. We all had a great dinner together, and then, when it was dark, Dan, our kids, Oliver, Bob, and I headed back to the beach to swim with the *Noctiluca*. When we arrived, we encountered two beach guards who told us to leave. Dan explained to them that we were doing scientific research (a bit of a stretch), and they left us alone to swim and wave our limbs gleefully as the *Noctiluca* lit up and sparkled in the bioluminescent sea.

Oliver and Bob left very early the next morning, and I received a letter dated two days later.

OLIVER SACKS, M.D.

2 HORATIO ST. #3G · NEW YORK, NY · 10014
TEL: 212.633.8373 · FAX: 212.633.8928
MAIL@OLIVERSACKS.COM   August 15, 05

Dear Sue and Dan,

That was a lovely weekend—Bob and I enjoyed ourselves
immensely (I hope we were not too difficult as guests).

I have been re-working the paper a bit—incorporating
your suggestions (and often your words), as well as making
other small changes—enlarging the early history of
stereoscopy (which one could enlarge much farther still, but
this would be out of scale with the rest), and (as you see)
inserting the lovely <u>Noctiluca</u> experience. So here it is once
again—I am tempted now to send it to my editor at <u>The
New Yorker</u>.

Then Oliver asked me if I wanted him to change my name to a
pseudonym and added "personally I like 'Stereo Sue,' but would not
want to embarrass you or cause offence." I don't think I ever told
Oliver just how much I loved the name Stereo Sue—it had bounce
to it and a rhythm that mimicked the famous opening measure of
Beethoven's Fifth!

A Small, Personal Triumph

In September 2005, while finishing up "Stereo Sue," Oliver sent me a letter with news and a question.

OLIVER SACKS, M.D.

2 HORATIO ST. #3G · NEW YORK, NY · 10014
TEL: 212.633.8373 · FAX: 212.633.8928
MAIL@OLIVERSACKS.COM

Sept 28/05

Dear Sue,

Kate and I have just got back from Europe—happy, jet-lagged, and facing a gigantic stack of mail (and an even larger one of email).

But among this I have a lovely letter from David Hubel, who liked the piece very much, and had interesting and important comments (tho' he, with his typical modesty, calls them unimportant, and adds "you should not change anything"). I am going up to Boston in a couple of days, will have lunch with him, and present "Stereo Sue" to the Mind, Brain and Behavior group.

I paused in my reading at this point. This was the first time my story would become a case history, discussed by neuroscientists who did not know me. I was a neuroscientist, too, but now I was also a patient—a confusing and not entirely comfortable position to be in.

. . .

But one question I am unclear about—and am reminded by as I get my morning stereo "fix" from <u>Hidden Depth</u> (the book of autostereograms compiled by Harry Storey). Do <u>you</u> "get" autostereograms (if you do, this suggests you would get random dot stereograms also), because some of these (at least) are purely abstract dots like random dot stereograms. Specifically, do you get <u>these</u>?

Otherwise, this is just a "hello" letter—a "thank you" again for your hospitality, the sheer pleasure of Woods Hole—and my best wishes to <u>all</u> of you.

Right away I sent an email, which included an answer to his question:

I do see depth in the simple wallpaper autostereograms. These are the stereograms where a figure is repeated across a horizontal row, then a different figure is repeated across the horizontal row below it, and so on. In most of these autostereograms, each row is at a different depth, but in some, different figures within a row can also be at different depths. I find these wallpaper autostereograms easy (and quite thrilling) to see probably because I practice convergent and divergent fusion regularly.

But my email didn't satisfy Oliver. He wanted to know if I could see the images in random dot stereograms and Magic Eye autostereograms because the images in these stereograms can only be seen if one has stereopsis. So, on October 10, 2005, I sent Oliver six stereograms from one of the Magic Eye books. Since I wanted to be completely honest with Oliver about my vision, I went into detail about what I saw. For one of the Magic Eye pictures (see insert photo 1), for example, I wrote,

> I see the two heads quite well and the right head, which is in profile, is in front of the left forward-facing head. Dan tells me that he can also see features, e.g., eyes, on the heads. I don't see these features, but the heads do emerge from the picture plane.

I added that when I see the 3D images in these stereograms, "I get a certain thrill, as if an electric shock ran through my body, and I feel like I am floating above the picture."

At the end of my letter, I also enclosed a special gift for Oliver, a beautiful photo of a squid embryo, twelve days after fertilization and 2.4 millimeters long, taken by my friend Karen Crawford* (see insert photo 2).

---

* In my letter, I also added the following: "Karen carries around in her head an entire three-dimensional atlas of the squid embryo, which she can mentally rotate and manipulate at will. She is also a very strong swimmer. We swam several times per week this summer and had some wonderful and wild ocean swims together. Karen is also the most visually aware person I know. She's always the first to spot the osprey flying overhead or the small fish jumping out of the water because of a feeding frenzy below, and when we comb the beach together, looking for sea glass, she finds five pieces to my one." Today, eighteen years after I wrote that letter, Karen continues to study squid development. She and her colleagues were the first to apply the CRISPR technique to squid embryos using a technically difficult procedure that Karen pioneered. See K. Crawford et al., "Highly efficient knockout of a squid pigmentation gene," *Current Biology* 30, no. 17 (September 2020): 3484–90.

Oliver's attention to my story, his trust in my descriptions, now gave me the confidence to think about writing my own book, a book that could go into far more detail about binocular vision, strabismus, vision therapy, and neuronal plasticity than Oliver's "Stereo Sue." I was planning on taking a sabbatical from teaching to write it. When I mentioned this to Oliver in an email dated Oct 14, his reaction could not have been more positive.

OLIVER SACKS, M.D.

2 HORATIO ST. #3G · NEW YORK, NY · 10014   Oct 17, 05
TEL: 212.633.8373 · FAX: 212.633.8928
MAIL@OLIVERSACKS.COM

Dear Sue,

A (relatively) short letter in response to your splendid one of the 14th[*] (but I am beset with the "closing" of another piece at <u>The New Yorker</u>—a piece on aphasia etc, after which they—and I—will turn to "your" piece—and most of my thoughts at the moment, are on music and the brain, which I am writing about).

First, thank you for the <u>wonderful</u> photo of the squid embryo, it's really exquisite, and I have put it up on my cephalopod door, next to some other spectacular teuthian[†] pictures. Thank you too for sending me the "MAGIC EYE" autostereograms which you get (I have already added something about his—and the history of such "illusions").

Thank you (in your previous letter) for retailing Theresa Ruggiero's excellent comments—I will reflect on these, and incorporate them when I get proofs of the piece.

---

[*] Oliver was referring to my email of Oct. 14, not a physical letter.

[†] Oliver was being creative again when he came up with the adjective "teuthian," from the word *teuthis*, a genus of squid.

And the BIG news is that you are thinking of a stereo-sabbatical! No one (experientially) is in a better position than yourself to tackle the subject of human visual plasticity and the possibility of obtaining stereovision in adult life—and as a neurobiologist you will bring all your professional skills as well to bear. Should be a winning combination!

I will write more soon but am pressed now.

And, then, about one month later, I eliminated all doubts about whether or not I could see with stereopsis as I described in my next letter, dated November 25, 2005:

The other day, November 23rd to be precise, I saw a random dot stereogram for the first time. I was reading Bela Julesz's book, *Foundations of Cyclopean Perception*, and I looked for the hundredth time at the color anaglyph of his basic RDS,* Fig. 2.4.1. (I've enclosed a color Xerox of this anaglyph.) I thought the central area of the central square was floating above the surround, although the sensation was not compelling. Unconvinced, I went into the kitchen, made myself a cup of tea, put the red-green lenses back on, and looked again at the anaglyph. This time, the central part of the central square receded quite a bit behind the surround, and the perimeter of the central square slanted upward toward the surround. Surprised, I wondered why the depth had reversed, but when I took off the red-green lenses, I realized that I had switched the lenses so that the green, not the red, lens was over my right eye. This fortuitous mistake convinced me that I really was seeing a random dot stereogram.

* RDS is an acronym for random dot stereogram. An example of an RDS is included here as insert photo 4.

I described how, with practice, the hidden square was standing out better and better in depth and that my breakthrough may have resulted from recent vision therapy exercises that were designed to reduce the vertical disparity between my two eyes. I ended the letter by writing,

> In your last letter, you mentioned that you are now writing about music and the brain. I hesitated before composing this letter because I did not want to intrude on your thoughts. However, I could not resist sending you a note describing this small, personal triumph.
>
> I hope you had a great Thanksgiving.

                              Stereo Sue

OLIVER SACKS, M.D.
2 HORATIO ST. #3G · NEW YORK, NY · 10014
TEL: 212.633.8373 · FAX: 212.633.8928
MAIL@OLIVERSACKS.COM

                                        December 13, 05

Dear Sue,

I should have answered your fascinating letter (of Nov 25) more promptly—but I have been preoccupied writing (mostly about music).

I thought you were getting there, with the autostereograms—and now <u>you</u> are there, extracting figures from quite difficult, fine-grain RDS—nice that the fortuitous error with the red-green glasses served to bring the new perception home, to <u>convince</u> you. This must be very satisfying (and a real source of fun!) and a testament to how well you are minimizing whatever vertical misalignment you still have.

I will, of course, include what you call "this small, personal triumph" in the piece—it is this, and more: it is the final ne plus ultra, or summa bonum (all these tags!) of stereoscopy. At present the piece is still with <u>The New Yorker</u>—and they will move on it in their own, unpredictable (and not to be hurried) time—when they <u>do</u> move, they move fast. So far (or did I mention this?) they have only sent their artist to see me, to look at stereo-paraphernalia, old stereo books, and glyphs etc. (I <u>hope</u>, but it is a slender hope, that they might have a special anaglyphic issue, for the first time.)

What an eventful year! My warmest wishes to you, to you all, for Christmas and the New Year.

An Ominous End to the Year

Oliver's letter was dated December 13, 2005, and postmarked on the 14th. Three days later, Oliver noticed a large blind spot and scintillations in his right eye. These were the first signs of a tumor on his retina caused by a cancer that would eventually blind his right eye and then kill him ten years later. While I was experiencing remarkable improvements in my vision, Oliver was losing his.

Unaware of his visual struggles, I sent Oliver a New Year's letter on December 29, 2005, with an amateurish red/green anaglyph of a cycad (one of his favorite plants) that I had made, with my son's help, using a simple anaglyph computer program (see insert photo 3).

I also described my visual adventures on a recent trip to Manhattan.

Last week, I was in New York City for my cousin's daughter's bat mitzvah. I took the train from Massachusetts into Penn Station and then the subway uptown to 72nd and Broadway. (This was before the transit workers' strike.) When I emerged from the subway station into the light of day, I had one of those moments of utter surprise and glee. The tall buildings looked so different; I felt like I was seeing them from an exaggerated perspective. One building across the street had a rounded facade that appeared to bulge out toward me.

Similarly, if I stood directly opposite the right-angle corner of a building, the corner loomed out dramatically. The buildings' brick facades were amazing—incredibly textured and detailed, with gargoyles and intricate designs. As I strolled along the streets with my cousins, I wanted to cry out about the spatial arrangements of branches on grand old trees and the detailed brickwork on lovely old buildings, but I held my tongue. Sometimes, when I start talking about my 3D revelations, I don't know when to stop.

Wishing you a very joyful new year.

Spatially yours,

Stereo Sue

Oliver wrote back promptly.

OLIVER SACKS, M.D.   January 5, 06
2 Horatio Street, 3G
New York, NY 10014
Tel: (212) 633-8373
Fax: (212) 633-8928

Dear Sue,

Thank you, thank you, for the lovely stereo-CYCAD—and yes, it does seem sinfully easy compared to what one used to do in "the old days" (a long-extinct process called CARRO, by which one made red-and-green diapositives, then superimposed these on a glass slide). It works beautifully— the choice of colors exactly right for some of the blue/red glasses I have—(perhaps cyan, rather than blue).

And what a beautiful, dramatic description of Manhattan, as seen through the now-coordinated eyes of a new-born stereope—

"Stereope," like "teuthobilia" in a former letter, were words Oliver made up, but he probably didn't know that *stereope* was actually a *real* word, a name for a type of fish. I told him that in my next letter, dated January 27, 2006, though most of the letter described how much more I could see while moving, how the combination of stereopsis and relative motion made the branches on trees stand out in dramatic depth.

═══

It was only when I read Oliver's book *The Mind's Eye* in 2010 that I realized the timing of the events of these few weeks. My December letter with the cycad anaglyph and my January letter with descriptions of my visual epiphanies arrived only a few weeks after Oliver was diagnosed with ocular melanoma. During that time he also underwent surgery to irradiate the tumor in his eye. Yet, in his January 5 letter, he did not mention his visual struggles. I now realized what the closing remarks in his letter must have meant to him: "This has been quite a year. I wonder what 2006 will bring?"

On February 16, 2006, Oliver sent a letter answering an email I had sent on that same day with a question about the wording in a recent draft of "Stereo Sue." A misplaced comma in the text had altered the meaning of one of the sentences. Again, he did not mention his cancer, but he typed this letter using a larger font with all capital letters.

OLIVER SACKS, M.D.
2 HORATIO ST. #3G · NEW YORK, NY · 10014
TEL: 212.633.8373 · FAX: 212.633.8928
MAIL@OLIVERSACKS.COM

2/16/06

DEAR SUE,

MANY THANKS FOR YOUR E-MAIL OF TODAY - ALWAYS GOOD TO HEAR FROM YOU !

I WAS BEWILDERED WHEN I SAW THE (NONSENSICAL) PHRASE - ZEUGMA, IF YOU WILL - " OPTICAL BEHAVIOUR " ; I FIND THIS COMES FROM A ~~MISREADING, OR PERHAPS A MIS-TRANSMISSION OF THE ORIGINAL TEXT, WHICH READ~~ --- A SLIGHT MISHAP IN OUR TEXT, ALLIED TO THE NON-TRANSMISSION OF A COMMA --- IT SHOULD READ " .. GIVEN THE APPROPIATE OPTICAL, BEHAVIOURAL OR SURGICAL HELP... ". WHATEVER WAS SAID THERE CAN EASILY BE CLARIFIED AND REFINED IN SUBSEQUENT DRAFTS/ PROOFS - AND, AS KATE INDICATED TO YOU, THERE MAY BE MANY OF THESE ...

I DID, SUBSEQUENTLY, MAKE SOME CHANGES TO THE OCT 6 DRAFT - CHANGES WHICH I HAVE NOT SENT TO THE NEW YORKER YET, BECAUSE I DON'T WANT TO MUDDLE THEM, AND I NEED TO GET THEIR FIRST PROOF, WITH ITS SUGGESTIONS AND EMENDATIONS, BEFORE I ADD ANYTHING NEW. BUT I DID MENTION IN IT THAT YOU HAVE NOW ADVANCED TO ' GETTING ' RDS - THE NE PLUS ULTRA OF STEREOSCOPY. (I ALSO SHORTENED AND CLAIFIED THE SLIGHTLY MUDDLY PARAGRAPH ABOUT N AUTOSTEREOGRAMS). ~~I WILL SNEB THIS ALONG~~ I WILL PROBABLY SEND THIS ALONG WHEN I HAVE A PROOF WHICH CAN GO WITH IT. .. I HOPE YOU ARE WELL.. AND YES, AN INCREDIBLE SPRING-LIKE DAY ! *Oliy*

At the time I wondered if his typewriter had gotten stuck in all-capitals mode. But the real reason was more ominous; it was getting harder for Oliver to read small print.

2 Horatio Street, #3G

On March 10, 2006, I came to Manhattan to see a Broadway play with Dan and my cousins. Before the play, I visited Oliver at his office apartment in Greenwich Village, at the very address to which I sent all my letters. After the building's doorman announced my arrival, I rode the elevator up to Oliver's floor, and Kate, whom I met for the first time that day, was at the main office door to greet me. Then, speaking loudly, she told Oliver that I had arrived, and Oliver peaked out, looking very shy, from behind the door of his inner office. It was only years later that I realized that all these announcements of my arrival may have been necessary. Because of his lifelong face blindness, a condition he later described in his 2010 book *The Mind's Eye*, Oliver might not have recognized me even though we had recently seen each other on two previous visits.

I joined Oliver in his inner office, where he sat at his desk and I on the sofa opposite. He gave me a book titled *Brewster on the Stereoscope*, written by Sir David Brewster and first published in 1856. I gave him Leonard Bernstein's book *The Unanswered Question* because I knew Oliver was writing about music. (I didn't know, however, until many letters later, that Oliver was not fond of Bernstein.) Oliver then calmly told me about his tumor. I must have looked horrified because he assured me that this cancer rarely metastasized and that he still had vision with his right eye and stereovision with both.

Shortly afterward, John Bennet, Oliver's *New Yorker* editor, joined us. I think Oliver and Kate had invited him so he could meet me, since I was the prime subject of Oliver's upcoming *New Yorker* piece. Bennet's subtle Texas accent surprised me. Somehow, I had not expected a *New Yorker* editor to speak with a slight southern drawl or to be so funny, as Bennet was when he told us a hilarious story about his Jack Russell terrier. Oliver told stories about the rivalry between Wheatstone and Brewster, who were inventors of the first stereoscopes, and then about jumping spiders, who have stereopsis and eight eyes. He picked up a piece of tungsten from his desk (additional elements and minerals crowded his desk and bookcase shelves) and had us feel its weight and listen to its sound. Then he disappeared briefly into the office's kitchen, reappearing with a delicious smoky tea, a mix of Darjeeling and Lapsang souchong, and letters and drawings from a gifted young man that Oliver wanted to show Bennet.

Shortly before I left, Kate brought out several plastic cuttlefish toys, and she and Oliver asked me to pick one out as a gift. When I hesitated, Oliver chose one for me—with the earnestness and care that one might expect of a seven-year-old boy, not a man in his seventies.

"Stereo Sue"

"Stereo Sue" finally appeared in *The New Yorker*'s June 19, 2006, issue. As is their custom, the print edition hit stands one week earlier, on Monday, June 12, but I didn't see a copy until June 13 because *The New Yorker* doesn't make its way to Western Massachusetts until the day after publication (and online versions were still in the future). I raced to the Odyssey Bookshop in South Hadley to buy multiple copies of the magazine. Oliver had quoted my first letter throughout the piece, and it was hard to believe that my own words were printed right there in *The New Yorker*. A large stereo pair spanned the first two pages, which I loved. I could fuse it, too, and see its depth. I wrote to Oliver right away. Since, at my visit to his office in March, Oliver assured me he still saw with stereopsis, I included a stereo pair at the top of the letter for him to free-fuse. But, knowing that he struggled with small print, I formatted the letter in 16-point font.

Source: John Walker, fourmilab.ch/cgi-bin/Solar*

June 19, 2006

Dear Oliver,

It was a real thrill to pick up a copy of the June 19 *New Yorker*
and see the words, "A Neurologist's Notebook" and "Stereo
Sue" in that very handsome and distinctive *New Yorker* font.
I am biased of course, but I think the story reads beautifully,
and I am enormously flattered that you included so many
quotes from my letters in your piece. Deep down, I never
really believed the story would be published, because if it
were, then this whole adventure would be too good to be
true. In fact, my stereo adventure—from the astonishing
change in my vision, to meeting and talking with you and
Kate, to *The New Yorker* story with its potential to help
others—this whole experience is to me like a very happy
fairy tale. Everyone should experience at least one such fairy
tale in their lifetime.

On the other hand, working with *The New Yorker* does
not always read like a fairy tale. I realize that it can be pretty
frustrating to extract definitive answers out of the editors,

---

* This image is meant to be free-fused with divergent fusion—that is, not by crossing
the eyes but by looking beyond the page.

but, as a reader, I've always enjoyed the great range of subjects discussed in the magazine. A few years ago, I had reason to like *The New Yorker* even more.

During the summer of 2002, my brother drove my parents out to Woods Hole to visit Dan, the kids, and me. We were renting the same funky old house on Bar Neck Road that we rented last summer. At that time, my mother had been living with Parkinson's disease for seventeen years, and she was quite physically disabled. The disease, however, had not touched her personality or intellect. My mother was a history professor, very learned, astute, and shrewd, but also unusually soft-spoken, tolerant, and nurturing. She read *The New Yorker* every week and always made sure that the *New Yorker* subscriptions for her three children were up-to-date.

One day during my parents' stay, numerous relatives and friends descended upon Woods Hole so that the house was overflowing with noise, food, and loud conversation. In the afternoon, however, the whole crowd left en masse for the beach, leaving my mother and me alone in a suddenly quiet house. My mother was feeling poorly that day, so I took her out into the sunshine on the deck off the kitchen. (Last summer, you stood by the steps to that deck studying with your monocular some lichen at your feet.) I settled my mother, all ninety pounds of her, in a chair, and put our small dog on her lap, since the dog's weight and warmth and sleepy contentment often calmed my mother's incessant tremors and dyskinesias.* I then picked up the most recent issue of *The New Yorker*, flipped to a long feature article, and began to read the story to her out loud. The article was about a man who had the uncanny ability to read people's thoughts and intentions by subtle changes in their facial

---

* Dyskinesias are involuntary, erratic movements that often occur after extended use of levodopa, the drug used to treat Parkinson's disease.

expressions.[*] I read the article slowly; my mother listened attentively, occasionally stopping me to comment on a passage. The afternoon passed in this pleasant way, with me reading and the dog snoring, and gradually, magically, my mother's body relaxed, her dyskinesias disappeared, and her movements became graceful and intentional. That is the happiest, the sweetest memory I have of my mother in her last difficult years, and I have had a warm feeling for *The New Yorker* ever since.

I want to end this letter by telling you just how much I appreciate your attention to my story, all of your writings, and your and Kate's friendship. It's hard to put these feelings into words, but here is a feeble attempt:

When our children were growing up, Dan and I read out loud to them as much as possible. We loved doing this. The first, real "chapter book" that we read to Jenny was *Charlotte's Web* by E. B. White. Like most very young children, Jenny wanted to hear the story over and over again, so that there was a period of time when Dan and I had practically the entire book memorized. I do not remember any of the details now, but I can still quote the closing lines. I read somewhere that White wrote the lines not just for Charlotte, the wise, talented, and heroic spider, but also for a good friend. On the assumption that you do not mind being likened to a fictional spider, substitute the words, "Oliver is" for "Charlotte was" in the last two sentences, and you have captured how I feel. The last lines read, "It is not often that someone comes along who is a true friend and a good writer. Charlotte was both."

Much love,

Stereo Sue

* The article was Malcolm Gladwell's "The Naked Face," published in *The New Yorker*, August 5, 2002.

P.S. The stereo pair on the first page is meant to be free-fused with "divergent" fusion. I hope that you can do this and that this doesn't frustrate you. You had mentioned that fusion was harder after your lateral rectus muscle was detached and reattached.

Oliver was away on a trip to Peru when I sent off my letter, but he responded with a handwritten note of his own a few weeks later. To thank him for the plastic cuttlefish toy, I had made him a flipbook by stapling together time-lapse images of a squid extending its tentacles.

OLIVER SACKS, M.D.

2 HORATIO ST. #3G · NEW YORK, NY · 10014
TEL: 212.633.8373 · FAX: 212.633.8928
MAIL@OLIVERSACKS.COM

July 14/06

Dear Sw,

I think I have written
about a hundred letters to
correspondents since 'SS' came out –
and nothing to you – Sorry!

Thank you very much. first,
for your charming flipbook
of an attacking squid – a
lovely idea ... I was very
taken by it –

And your few earlier letter
(q June 19) – we had already
left for PERU then – this too
was so thoughtful, so you,
from the stereo pair at the top

OLIVER SACKS, M.D.

2 HORATIO ST. #3G • NEW YORK, NY • 10014
TEL: 212.633.8373 • FAX: 212.633.8928
MAIL@OLIVERSACKS.COM

2)

to the F.B -
which transfer

at the end -

I was deeply moved too by your description of how your mother's parkinsonism + dyskinesias melted away as she became immersed in what you were reading - the power of engagement   (I have just been writing, too much, on the power(s) of music, not least in people with parkinsonism ...).

We will have to think what to do with scores of other letters - but I wanted to write this little personal letter first - and give my deepest thanks to you

OLIVER SACKS, M.D.
2 HORATIO ST. #3G · NEW YORK, NY · 10014
TEL: 212.633.8373 · FAX: 212.633.8928
MAIL@OLIVERSACKS.COM

3)

for being 'stereo-Sue',
so eloquent and so generous
with my fumbling attempts
to understand n describe.

I ~~think~~ We were
really collaborators, not
"investigator" and "subject" —
as it should be.

It was an unprecedented
experience for me as well.

Much love,

Olly

OLIVER SACKS, M.D.

2 HORATIO ST. #3G · NEW YORK, NY · 10014
TEL: 212.633.8373 · FAX: 212.633.8928
MAIL@OLIVERSACKS.COM

July 14, 2006

Dear Sue,

I think I have written almost a <u>hundred</u> letters to correspondents since "SS" came out—and nothing to you—sorry!

Thank you <u>very</u> much, first, for your charming flipbook of an attacking squid—a lovely idea—I was very taken by it.

And your fine earlier letter (of June 19)—we had already left for PERU then—this too was so thoughtful, so you, from the stereo pair at the top to the E. B. White transfer at the end.

I was deeply moved too by your description of how your mother's parkinsonism and dyskinesias melted away as she became immersed in what you were reading—the power of <u>engagement</u> (I have just been writing, this week, on the power(s) of music, not least in people with parkinsonism).

We will have to think what to do with <u>scores</u> of other letters—but I wanted to write this little personal letter first—and give my deepest thanks to <u>you</u> for being "Stereo-Sue," so eloquent and so generous with my fumbling attempts to understand and describe.

We were really collaborators, not "investigator" and "subject"—as it should be.

It was an unprecedented experience for me as well.

Much love,

Oliver

Just the Beginning

After "Stereo Sue" was published, I wondered if my friendship with Oliver would fade away. But I need not have worried. Oliver had already become a constant and stimulating presence in my life. Whenever I encountered something exciting or learned something new, I found myself composing a letter about it to Oliver in my head, and these thoughts often led to real words on paper. I simply couldn't stop writing to Oliver, and he, in turn, responded with his own musings and drafts of the material he was writing.

Moreover, the response to "Stereo Sue" was more than I had hoped or imagined. Oliver had given me a new name and identity, which, seventeen years later, I still carry. I had thought that if I could help just one cross-eyed person with my story, that would be enough. Yet, to date, I have received emails from more than one thousand people with visual conditions similar to my own. I had no idea how much "Stereo Sue" would resonate with others. But one of the first people to understand its impact was a journalist at National Public Radio.

Morning Edition

On April 27, two months before "Stereo Sue" appeared in *The New Yorker*, I got a surprise email from Robert Krulwich, a science reporter for National Public Radio (NPR). He wrote that he had been a friend of Oliver's and Kate's going "back a long, long way, to 'The Man Who Mistook His Wife' . . . days," and sometimes he did radio pieces about Oliver's tales. Oliver had shown him "Stereo Sue," and he thought it would make a nice story for NPR. For the piece, he wanted to interview Oliver and other people who seemed key to the story. "But first," he wrote to me, "I'd like to call. Can I?"

I am an avid NPR listener, so to have a science reporter from NPR ask if he could please call me was a thrill. Since I was going to be in Manhattan on May 15, we scheduled an interview at the NPR studios there. On the morning of the interview, I walked to the studio in a torrential downpour. After we shook hands, Robert suggested we grab a snack at the Dunkin Donuts across the street. Gesturing toward my sopping-wet umbrella, I pointed out that it was pouring outside. Undaunted, Robert dashed umbrella-less across the street while I followed more cautiously. As he enthusiastically gobbled down several donuts, he entertained me with a story about a college romance. I nervously picked at my donut at first, but Robert was so warm and funny, I began to relax, which was probably the whole point of the Dunkin Donuts foray.

Back in the studio, we settled into the recording room. Robert was well prepared for the interview, having read my original letter to Oliver and other material I had sent him, so I was surprised by his first question:

"What did you have for breakfast?"

"Bagel" was my one-word answer.

He asked me what I had with the bagel. Why this interest in my breakfast? "Just a bagel," I insisted. At this point, Robert told me he did not really care what I had for breakfast but that the sound engineers in the adjacent room needed to hear my voice. As Robert explained, most people are busy doing something else while listening to the radio, so the quality of our voices, to be heard and understood, must be excellent.

The interview went on for about forty-five minutes. After it was all over, we sat and talked casually for another hour. Robert later interviewed Oliver, Dr. Theresa Ruggiero, and Dr. David Hubel separately, but in the eight-minute piece that aired on *Morning Edition* June 26, 2006, "Going Binocular: Susan's First Snowfall," it sounds as though we were all together at one time having a conversation. That is the genius of Robert Krulwich.

Author, Author

"Dear Professor Barry: I hope that you are the person whose story regarding stereoscopic vision was related on NPR."

This was a common opening to many emails I received in the days after the *Morning Edition* program. My email address had not been made public, but people found me anyway. Almost all of the emails were from individuals seeking help for their vision. Other people wrote to Oliver. Indeed, five days after the NPR program aired, Kate sent an email addressed to me, Robert Krulwich, and John Bennet. It read,

> Wow. Tremendous feedback from both *The New Yorker* and the NPR piece on stereo. I am wading through scores of emails and snail mails, some of which I will sort and pass on to Sue and Theresa R.
>
> I think it's very clear there are thousands of people out there who are quite personally affected by this, not to mention many others who are intellectually intrigued by it as well. And of course all those closet stereo buffs.

Those emails and letters further motivated me to research and write a book of my own. "Most of my books have started out as letters to colleagues or friends," Oliver wrote to me, and I was using my letters to Oliver in just this way. As I wrote, I worked out problems and fleshed out ideas, many of which ended up in my book. Oliver encouraged me to talk with other people like myself. I did, and wrote to him all about them. Oliver replied kindly, thanking me for my "very full" letters and describing briefly the work he was doing on his much larger, eighth book, *Musicophilia*, about the power of music to move, heal, and sometimes haunt us.

═══

During my research, I met with Shinsuke Shimojo,[*] a scientist whom Oliver had consulted when researching "Stereo Sue." I included a description of my meeting in a letter dated December 29, 2006.

> I had a very nice lunch in Harvard Square with Shinsuke Shimojo. We went to a Vietnamese restaurant and talked about stereovision the whole time. (Shortly into the meal, Dr. Shimojo did tell me to give up on chopsticks and use a fork.) He also told me that when he first read a draft of "Stereo Sue," he wasn't sure he believed the story, but after talking with me, he was convinced of the validity of my case. He said something else that I thought was very nice. He said that he decided to study perception after seeing a Julesz random dot stereogram. Now that he is an established scientist with a big lab and grants to write, some of the magic has been taken away from doing the research. When he read the first draft that you sent him of "Stereo Sue," he was reminded of why he went into perceptual research in the first place.

In Oliver's letter, dated January 6, 2007, he responded in his usual encouraging way.

---

[*] Shinsuke Shimojo is the Gertrude Baltimore Professor of Experimental Psychology at the California Institute of Technology. He studies human perception, cognition, and action.

I'm delighted you were able to have lunch with Shinsuke—and
I burst out laughing when I read how he had suggested you
let the chopsticks go and use a fork. When I first met him he
spoke very movingly of Julesz, but I did not get the impression
that the magic had been taken away. Well, perhaps some of
it—maybe it has to go as one focusses in on a problem, and
then comes back when, the problem solved, one can now see
everything in a broader/deeper perspective. Certainly none of
the magic of stereoscopy has evaporated for you—and I think
it will provide an essential excitement all through your book
(as it does in every letter you write).

Through Oliver's writings, he taught me that an understanding
of a disease or disorder requires a very broad approach, including the scientific, psychological, historical, and philosophical. The
same of course was true for strabismus. People with misaligned
eyes face a serious perceptual problem. Since the eyes are pointing
to different regions in space, they provide uncorrelated input to
the brain. How does one create a single view of the world from
this conflicting input? Each person with strabismus addresses this
problem with their own combination of adaptations and compen-
sations. So, to understand strabismus, I had to research not only
scientific studies on binocular vision but also the different ways
people coped or rehabilitated themselves. Just as Oliver had visited
me at my home, I traveled to different eye doctors to talk with
them and their patients.* And I found some of the best writing
on strabismus in an obscure journal—*The Optometric Weekly* of

* The optometrists I visited and consulted, in addition to Dr. Ruggiero, included Drs. Ken
Ciuffreda, David Cook, Nathan Flax, Amiel Francke, Ray Gottlieb, Israel Greenwald, Carl
Gruning, Paul Harris, Carl Hillier, Caroline Hurst, Hans Lessman, Dennis Levi, Robin
Lewis, Brenda Montecalvo, Leonard Press, Robert Sanet, Cathy Stern, John Streff, Selwyn
Super, Barry Tannen, and Nancy Torgerson. I also benefited from conversations with
several vision therapists, including Michelle Dilts, Diana Ludlam, Ellen Middleton, Linda
Sanet, and Laurie Sadowski.

the 1940s and '50s. In weekly installments, the optometrist Frederick W. Brock had outlined a vision training program for strabismus. I became fascinated with the man and his work and described all this to Oliver in my letter of December 29, 2006.

What I really wanted to write to you about, however, is a relatively unknown optometrist named Frederick W. Brock. I sent you a Brock string a year and a half ago. This device, several beads that can slide along a string, is as powerful as it is simple. It teaches the patient to fixate both eyes on the same point in space. How do you know if you are using both eyes and if your eyes are pointing at the same place? You know because, if you do the exercise properly, you will see a symmetrical double string image coming into and out of the fixated bead. It took me a full year to master a three-bead, five-foot-long string, and it was one of the most effective procedures that I performed.

The Brock string is only one of many procedures that Dr. Brock developed to promote binocular vision in strabismics. All of his devices are simple, elegant, and effective, and he built all of these gadgets himself.

. . .

So I got very curious about Frederick Brock. What got him interested in strabismus? Was he a kind and decent person? Dr. Brock died in 1972 so I will never meet him. I did, however, experience the second-best thing. I went down to the SUNY College of Optometry on 42nd St. in Manhattan to meet with Dr. Israel Greenwald, who was Dr. Brock's protégé and later his partner in private practice. When I mentioned to Dr. Greenwald that I thought Brock was a sort of genius concerning strabismus, Dr. Greenwald said, "Yes, and he was the nicest of men, too." Dr. Greenwald spent hours with me showing me Brock's procedures and provided me with a complete list of Brock's writings and papers. I spent the next day copying many of the papers from the SUNY library.

. . .

As I made my way home on the train, I read one of the papers detailing procedures to help strabismics. . . . Imagine my surprise when, in this paper, Brock wrote, "It must be repeated here that, before stereopsis is actually experienced by the patient, there is nothing one can do or say which will adequately explain to him the actual sensation experienced in stereoscopic vision. It is, therefore, very important that the patient believes he is looking at just another two-dimensional chart, and it must be left to him to discover, with utter amazement, that the chart assumes stereoscopic properties. In this way, and only in this way, can we be sure that stereopsis is really obtained. Once the patient has experienced this new sensation, he is only too anxious to use it again and again until it is surely and definitely established."

Boy, does this sound familiar! This was exactly my experience and also the experience of other formerly stereoblind people that I have interviewed.

. . .

Dr. Brock performed lots of perceptual experiments on his patients and asked them what it was that they saw. From these observations and discussions, he devised his therapy procedures and devices. Dr. Brock was not content to look at his patients from the outside, but, like Chesterton's Father Brown,[*] a character you quote in *An Anthropologist on Mars*, Brock wanted to get inside his patients' heads.

---

[*] G. K. Chesterton wrote fifty-three short stories about a fictional Roman Catholic priest named Father Brown, who used his deep understanding of human nature to solve many crimes.

You begin your book *A Leg to Stand On* with a quote from Montaigne: ". . . to become a true doctor, a man must have experienced all the illnesses he hopes to cure . . ." However, one would be wary of an ophthalmic surgeon who had strabismus and poor stereopsis. Most strabismics, then, are treated by doctors who have no personal experience with their condition. What about Dr. Brock? What gave him his insights? Perhaps, you have guessed the punchline already. Dr. Brock *was* a strabismic, an intermittent exotrope.* The first patient that he treated was himself.

Oliver's response to my stories was filled with his usual exuberant use of adjectives and parentheses, but the news in his letter of January 6, 2007, about his own vision was alarming.

Thanks very much for your grand letter (of 12/29), crackling with intellectual energy and enthusiasm. The Brock stuff sounds very important, almost prescient—and, apparently, virtually unknown. You will do a great service exhuming it (and him), bringing it (and him) to life again. It may be worth a separate essay, sometime, as well as a chapter in your book. And this, you say, is all but complete!

(I thought my book was "all but complete" two months ago—but I have since had hundreds of afterthoughts, and have revised many chapters radically—I hope for their good, and not out of mischief.)

You raise a very deep question about what a doctor/scientist needs to have experienced in his own person. . . . The strength—but to some extent the narrowness—of my coming MUSIC book is that so much of it consists of reports from the hallucinated, the amusic, the synesthetic etc, those who know, from their

---

* Exotropia is a form of strabismus in which one eye deviates outward.

own experience, what it is like—but can also, to some extent, stand outside it. If the hallucinator (or whatever) is also a professional scientist, or physician, or analyst—that is an unbeatable combination. This, of course, is your combination. And with various forms of visual impairment and interference, mine too. (I seem to live now in a <u>braided</u> world, with twists and warps which the left eye cannot fully correct, so, increasingly, I close or (somehow) "suppress" the distorted and compromised vision of the right eye—and this, in turn, predisposes to de-afferentation hallucinations—I find all this very interesting, and record it carefully, but I do wish it wasn't happening to me.)

. . .

The important thing, at the moment, is that I have been able to work hard, consistently, enthusiastically, and productively. And almost to exhaustion. I will take off for a few days (swimming) around the 17th. Again, congratulations on your expanding exciting work, and the best of New Years to you all.

Oliver had lost what I had gained, stereovision, but, more than that, he was living in a visually distorted world. I felt I had to do something. We both strongly believed in the powers of rehabilitation, so a few months later, I sent him a huge box full of objects for exercises that could improve his ability to navigate the world with just one eye. I don't think he ever did the exercises. He was too busy writing the voluminous *Musicophilia*, but he appreciated the gesture. At that point and many times in the future, I was struck by his ability to keep working, to keep pushing past whatever obstacles were in his path. "The important thing, at the moment," he had written, "is that I have been able to work hard, consistently, enthusiastically, and productively."

Throughout 2007, I continued to send updates on my research for
my book. On July 9, I wrote,

> I've mentioned to you that I've been impressed with the work
> and writings of an optometrist named Frederick Brock. Brock
> was heavily influenced by a physician named Goldstein,
> who wrote a book called *The Organism*. I had never heard of
> Goldstein, and the title of his book sounded old-fashioned,
> but I decided I had better track the book down. This turned
> out to be easy, as my college library had two editions. I picked
> the 1995 edition off the shelf only to find that you had written
> the foreword. In fact, you stated, "Kurt Goldstein is one of the
> most important, most contradictory, and now most forgotten
> figures in the history of neurology and psychiatry."
>
> Brock felt that the only way to get a strabismic to see like a
> normal viewer was to present them with a task that was within
> their capabilities but could be achieved only by using both eyes.
> This reminded me of your story of Madeleine J. in the chapter
> "Hands" in your *Hat* book*—of how you gently tricked her into
> using her hands. I was very moved by that story—of her
> discovery of a skill that she thought was beyond her.

This was a very long letter, but I finally, hesitantly, brought it to a
close with a request.

> This brings me to the part of the letter in which I want to ask you a
> question. Would you be willing to write the foreword to my book?

---

* In the story "Hands," Oliver described an elderly woman he called Madeleine J. who was blind and
had cerebral palsy. She was very intelligent but had been so thoroughly cared for all her life, she had
never learned to use her hands. She thought they were useless "lumps of dough." When Oliver found
that her hands had normal sensations, he instructed her nurses to put her food, a bagel, slightly
beyond her grasp so that she would have to use her hands to grasp it. This she did and, in so doing,
discovered not only the bagel but her hands. She began to explore everything through touch, asked
for clay, and began to sculpt, displaying an artistic talent no one would have guessed she had. "Who
would have dreamed that basic powers of perception," Oliver wrote, "normally acquired in the first
months of life, but failing to be acquired at this time, could be acquired in one's sixtieth year?"

I waited nervously for Oliver's response, which arrived in a letter dated August 25, 2007. It was written with a big, sloppy hand.

OLIVER SACKS, M.D.   8/25/07

2 HORATIO ST. #3G · NEW YORK, NY · 10014
TEL: 212.633.8373 · FAX: 212.633.8928
MAIL@OLIVERSACKS.COM

Dear Sue,

Belated thanks (I have been away) for your super-letter (of the 9th). My typewriter is broken, my hand-writing slow (and, I am told, "difficult") so a short, preliminary reply.

Belated thanks (I have been away) for your super-letter (of the 9th). My typewriter is broken, my hand-writing slow (and, I am told, "difficult") so a short, <u>preliminary</u> reply.

He then went on to say that he would defer comment on the main substance of my long letter—"I see that you are bubbling with ideas!" but added, "and simply say, at this point, that I would be delighted to write a foreword to your book. I will write again soon."

On October 5, 2008, I sent Oliver a draft of *Fixing My Gaze*, but, shortly afterward, realized I made a terrible mistake. By this time, the book had been reviewed by my editor at Basic Books, who had done a thorough and excellent job, encouraging me to tell my story (with a few exceptions) in chronological order, eliminating repetition, and reminding me not to "berate the reader." But we had one serious disagreement. I had written about Oliver's role in my story, and she had removed those paragraphs. I put them back in, and she took them out again. She was concerned that Oliver's voice would overwhelm my own and reasoned that readers would learn of Oliver's contribution through his foreword and my acknowledgments. So the draft I sent to Oliver did not include a word about his contribution. He never mentioned this in the letter he wrote back to me—yet another reminder of his generous nature.

OLIVER SACKS, M.D.

2 HORATIO ST. #3G · NEW YORK, NY · 10014
TEL: 212.633.8373 · FAX: 212.633.8928
MAIL@OLIVERSACKS.COM

Monday, Oct 13, 08

Dear Sue,

I have your in-all-ways beautifully clear text—and your very nice letter of the 5th.

I read the book at once—easy to do because the narrative is gripping, and the interleaving with exposition, discussion, and of course, others' experiences—is so natural and seamless. Many things occurred to me as I read—first how much more than stereopsis was affected (flickering, lack of visual continuity, difficulty of holding fixation, relative lack of peripheral awareness, etc etc); how difficult, for example, driving was—at least, how complicated. You did not lay much stress on these "other" problems when we met (and I did not stress them in STEREO SUE), and it may be that only in retrospect, and as you reflect, does the whole picture emerge. Certainly there was "accommodation"—but you had a lot to accommodate to: and, as you bring out, there were often perceptual and other "costs" to accommodation.

Your end-notes and bibliography—half the length of the text itself!—is quite amazing: almost a supplementary book in itself (as a footnote person, this is very much to my taste) and it will provide academic readers with all the references they need—one of the many excellences of your book, of course, is that it addresses "simple" readers—in particular, readers who have eye problems of their own, and academic ones, equally.

Beyond the specifics, the theme of plasticity runs through the book. I like the way you introduce it with Dan (tho' the chronology of some of your thinking, as you related in Ch 1, puzzles me a bit: you wonder if you can change the way you see the world, the circuitry in your visual cortex (pp. 19, 21) but end by saying that you would have thought the acquisition of stereo by an adult impossible, in 2001).[*] That you achieved and that, potentially, a great many people with similar problems can hope for change, is the essential "good news" of the book, the good news made possible by plasticity.

But, equally, you stress the importance of a wise, detailed, stage-by-stage regimen suggested and supervised by a behavioural optometrist—what you describe here in the book is MUCH more complex than I originally thought, and occupied several months (did it not?); (incidentally your discussion of BROCK here was of very great interest—he seems to have foreseen and done so much) the detailed regimen AND (no less important!) the time, the care, the efforts, the patience, the determination, the tenacity, the

---

* This was clarified in the final book version.

intelligence which the subject/patient/client (don't know what word to use) must put out for themselves. (Theresa Ruggiero always said that while your ocular/strabismic problems were common, your determination to work and change, the patience etc, was far from common.)

How much accommodation is "automatic," how much training, discipline, tenacity, individual action and resourcefulness—you already bring out in the analogy with Dan—and this came up when we first met, at his 1996 launch party.

I think you have written a really important, very clear and (equally crucial!) a very <u>balanced</u> book.

I made some notes and sketched a foreword as soon as I read it—but I must make a second more careful reading now—do what I can to bring out its very special importance—and quality.

Let's stay in close touch—

I felt so bad about the draft I sent him that I could not revel in his glowing letter. Fortunately, Oliver phoned me a few days later, which gave me a chance to recount my discussions with my editor and her reasons for removing him from my book. Oliver told me that he had wondered why I had not mentioned him but understood my editor's concerns. A few days earlier, however, I had sent an impassioned email to my editor who responded by reminding me that her comments were suggestions, not ultimatums, so I was able to tell Oliver that I had already put him back into my story.

But Oliver had phoned for another reason. He felt that, in our initial talks and correspondence, I had downplayed the difficulties caused by my crossed eyes. His remarks got me thinking: How much can people, in general, attribute their problems to a childhood disorder and how should they weigh the advice or comments given by their doctors or other people who do not live with the disorder? I tried to answer Oliver's question in my next letter.

Oct. 19, 2008

Dear Oliver,

Thanks so much for reading my book and drafting a foreword. I really enjoyed our phone conversation last week and have been thinking about your questions.

You asked me why I did not initially mention to you the problems that I encountered with school, driving, and other activities. Why had I misled you? (You didn't put it that way, but that's the question I asked myself.) I mentioned over the phone that I did not want to exaggerate my circumstances. Although I had real troubles learning to read, I eventually became a good student. At the time I was growing up, girls were not required or expected to play ball sports, so I attributed my clumsiness to being a girl. I did wonder if my fear of driving was connected to my vision but decided it was more closely linked with a general dislike for going fast and a cautious, fearful nature. In short, the main reason that I downplayed my difficulties was that I did not always connect them with my vision.

When you suggested in an early letter to me that I seek out other strabismic people, I thought to myself that I did not need a "support group" and did not want to hang around with people who had crossed eyes. I did not change my mind about this until after you published "Stereo Sue" and Robert Krulwich aired his *Morning Edition* story about me. Since that time, I have received 333 emails specifically from strabismics and amblyopes.* Most of my correspondents are not seeking the magical experience of seeing in stereo but instead are searching for ways to make their everyday lives easier, to see with less effort. They had all been told by their doctors that they were fine and that their vision was more than adequate. I had been told the same thing: Dr. Fasanella had said to me that I could do anything except fly an airplane.

I expect that Dr. Fasanella as well as most of my correspondents' doctors were trying to be encouraging and reassuring, but these doctors may also have been ignorant of what their patients were experiencing. While reading all the emails, I realized that having strabismus, though certainly not a tragic situation, did indeed present some difficulties, and I began to reevaluate my own experiences and think about writing a book. As I began to investigate strabismus, I started to understand what Theresa Ruggiero had been telling me—that my inability to bifixate and my poor sense of the visual periphery compromised my sense of where I and other things were in space.

Yet in this letter, I still held back. To paraphrase Oliver: We grow out of our childhood but never outgrow it.† As a young girl, I felt like a failure because of my crossed eyes and my ensuing struggles with reading, bicycling, and driving. I just didn't want to revisit all

---

* Strabismics refers to people with misaligned eyes while amblyopes refers to people with "lazy eye." Many people in these groups suffer from poor stereovision or are stereoblind.

† O. Sacks, "Humphry Davy: The Poet of Chemistry," originally published in *The New York Review of Books* (November 4, 1993), and later, in abridged form, in O. Sacks, *Everything in Its Place: First Loves and Last Tales* (New York: Alfred A. Knopf, 2019).

that. And I didn't want to complain to Oliver. After all, he had cared for patients, described in *Awakenings*, who had been physically and mentally immobilized for decades. Although my crossed eyes had a persistent and negative effect throughout my life, my difficulties seemed minor in comparison.

In the process of writing *Fixing My Gaze*, I finally revisited those childhood problems. When, in an early draft, I alluded to my troubles in school, my editor asked me to expand on the topic. I added a paragraph, but she demanded more. Eventually, I told the whole story. As my book went to print, I worried that people would think I had exaggerated. Instead, I received email after email from others with strabismus who wrote that, in describing my difficulties, I could have been writing about them.

Fixing My Gaze: A Scientist's Journey Into Seeing in Three Dimensions was published in May 2009. It was named one of the ten best science books of 2009 by the editors of Amazon.com and has been translated into eight languages. I gave talks about it around the US and in Canada, Brazil, and Europe. But most important, the book provided information and help to people with strabismus and other binocular vision disorders. The book was to my mind one of the best things I've ever done. While doing research for the book, I received excellent help and advice from Theresa Ruggiero, the whole community of behavioral and developmental optometrists,* and many scientists. Yet, without Oliver's support and encouragement, I'm not sure I would have written it.

---

* Two organizations founded by behavioral and developmental optometrists are the College of Optometrists in Vision Development (COVD; covd.org), whose name changed to Optometric Vision Development and Rehabilitation Association (OVDRA) in 2024, and the Optometric Extensions Program (oepf.org).

The Color of Words

Oliver and I discussed many topics beyond stereovision, often exchanging stories about the natural world. But at my first visit to his Greenwich Village office apartment on March 10, 2006, our conversation turned to music and synesthesia. I knew about synesthesia, I said to him, because I had it. Oliver was intrigued. Could I tell him more? Or better yet, write to him about it. Indeed, a letter seemed like the best idea. Oliver didn't hear all that well. He was constantly fussing with his hearing aids. During a single conversation, he might put them in, then take them out, then put them in again. Oliver had a great sense of humor and could be a lot of fun to talk to, but if I wanted to make sure he understood my words, it was better to put them in writing. Besides, writing a letter gave me the time to think about what I wanted to say. So, five days after my visit, I wrote the following letter.

March 15, 2006

Dear Oliver,

I had a wonderful time at your apartment last Friday. I was so glad to meet Kate and also John Bennet. I enjoyed

hearing stories about Wheatstone and Brewster,[*] feeling
the weight and hearing the sound of tungsten, and learning
about the many eyes of jumping spiders. (I just learned that
the amphibians *Xenopus laevis* have side-facing eyes as
tadpoles. However, during metamorphosis, the eyes move
forward for binocular vision. I wonder what wiring changes
occur in their brains.)

You asked me to write you a letter about synesthesia,
and I thought I had better write right away before I go away
on vacation next week. I think I have been a synesthete since
childhood, but I only discovered that I had synesthesia
maybe eight years ago. I was chatting with my neurobiology
students after a long afternoon in the lab, and we happened
to be talking about names that we would give our children. I
said that one should of course like the color of the name.
One of the students got quite interested in this remark and
asked me if I associated colors with anything else. I said that
I associated colors with letters, numbers, words, and proper
nouns, such as the names of people, months of the year, and
days of the week. My student had worked as a lab technician
for Dr. Ramachandran,[†] and she told me that I had
synesthesia, a phenomenon that he had studied. I was
skeptical and told her that I just made strong color
associations. She insisted that this was a real phenomenon
and said she would prove it to me.

---

[*] Charles Wheatstone (1802–75) and David Brewster (1781–1868) were both pioneers in
the field of binocular vision. Wheatstone invented the first stereoscope, although Brewster
created a more popular model. They had a fierce rivalry that was both scientific and personal.

[†] V. S. Ramachandran is a distinguished professor of psychology at the University of
California, San Diego, where he directs the Center for Brain and Cognition. He has
studied synesthesia, among his many other explorations of the human brain, and is the
author of several popular science books, including *Phantoms in the Brain*, *The Tell-Tale
Brain*, and *A Brief Tour of Human Consciousness*.

The next day, my student appeared in my office with a clipboard containing a list of words, letters, and numbers. She asked me to describe the colors I saw when she read the items on her list. I began to feel a bit silly when I told her in detail what I "saw." The letter "C" was snow white with pale pink overtones, the letter "N" was a beautiful yellow-brown, exactly the color and grain of an oak hardwood floor, while the letter "H" was a dark green, a damp letter evoking the chilly dankness of the scum you might find growing on a damp concrete wash basin in someone's basement. Words, I told her, often take on the same color as their first letter. For example, "S" is a green letter, and the word "synesthesia" starts out green but blends into a yellow-orange because the long E sound is yellow-orange. The number three is the color of young grass while thirteen has the color and taste of cooked spinach. Since I really like spinach, I like the number thirteen. My student also asked the same questions of five students and took careful notes. She returned with her clipboard two weeks later. I gave her exactly the same answers for all the items on her list while all her other subjects gave her random responses.

Two years ago, my brother and I were chatting about a high school English teacher when he mentioned to me that he had once written a story for English class about a man who saw colors with letters. It turns out that my brother also sees colors when he thinks of letters, although his colors are different from mine. When my brother and I were growing up, we had very different interests. My interests were in natural history, identifying rocks, trees, and wildflowers, while his passion was studying the French Revolution. However, as adults, our interests converged. We both independently discovered music theory and number theory, and we think about these subjects in the same way, using visual images. My brother's nine-year-old daughter is also a synesthete. She's a very creative, delightful little person, and I like sharing this oddity with her. We argue every time we're together about what colors go with what letters, words, and numbers.

I always see images when I hear music, but I do not associate specific colors with particular musical keys or musical intervals. I wish that I could say that a minor third is always a blue-green color, but I do not distinguish the intervals all that well. My musical skills are pretty modest. When I hear music, I see little circles or vertical bars of light getting brighter, whiter, or more silvery for higher pitches and turning a lovely deep, maroon for the low pitches. A run up the scale will produce a succession of increasingly brighter spots or vertical bars moving upward, while a trill, like in a Mozart piano sonata, will produce a flicker. High distinct notes on a violin evoke sharp bright lines while notes played with vibrato seem to shimmer. Several string instruments playing together evoke overlapping, parallel bars or, depending on the melody, spirals of light of different shades shimmering together. Sounds made by brass instruments produce a fan-like image. High notes are positioned slightly in front of my body, at head level, and toward the right while bass notes are located deep in the center of my abdomen. A chord will envelop me. I feel a little foolish writing all these things. This sounds nuts! But these experiences are always there with the music.

I do not see synesthetic images in stereoscopic depth. The images did not change when my vision transformed but remained stable and involuntary.

I had never thought to put a value on this synesthesia. On page 187 of *The Unanswered Question*, Bernstein encourages the listener to get rid of all that "synesthesia baggage" and just hear the music. I do not know if I can do that, and, frankly, I do not want to get rid of the imagery. In school, it was easier to memorize dates for history class because the dates had colors. However, my sister, who is not a synesthete, has a remarkable ability to memorize long lists of numbers, as did my grandfather. My sister can just see the whole list in her head. So synesthesia may help with visual memory, but it is certainly not essential for it. Synesthesia is just there. It enriches my visual imagery and my appreciation for music. I guess I really do like it.

The letter then turned to a further discussion of stereovision before I signed off with "Yours in every sense." When Oliver completed a draft of *Musciophilia* with a chapter on musical synesthesia, he sent me a draft of the chapter and wrote on November 16, 2006,

> I was amazed when you too turned out to be a synesthete and I quote you—I hope accurately—toward the end of the piece. I enclose what I have written. I will be happy to revise or correct (or add) anything in regard to your own experiences—and knowing (from "Stereo Sue") what an excellent feel you have for narrative, logic etc. etc. would also value your opinion on the piece as a whole.

I had no trouble with Oliver adding my experiences with synesthesia in his book, but I asked him not to identify me by my full name. I was afraid that people would think me crazy. If you look closely, however, you can find Oliver's description of my musical synesthesia in the "The Key of Clear Green: Synesthesia and Music," a chapter in *Musicophilia*.

Musical Interlude I

On January 21, 2007, I received an email from Kate saying that Oliver's music book was almost ready to be sent to the publishers. "Shall I send you a copy of it for reading fun?" I knew of Oliver's love and fascination with music. He had described in his memoir *Uncle Tungsten* how he grew up in a musical household and, in *Awakenings*, highlighted music's therapeutic powers. His father's beautiful Bechstein piano graced Oliver's living room. It was covered with the musical scores (xeroxed and enlarged) that Oliver regularly played.

Feb. 9, 2007

Dear Oliver,

Kate sent me a copy of your new book. It flew over cyberspace from her computer to mine in a fraction of a second, which is remarkable. I printed it out and read it and enjoyed it tremendously.

. . .

You mention that musicality tends to run in families, but your book makes us all wonder why some people are more sensitive to or gifted in music than others. During the last five months of my pregnancy with Andy, I did a little experiment. I played every night for the baby inside me a recording of Bach's double violin concerto in D minor. I very much like the piece in part because my brother and father played it together when I was growing up. When Andy was a very young infant, he seemed to recognize the concerto because he got very animated when he heard it, more excited than when he heard other music. However, I did not continue to play the piece for him regularly during his childhood. In fact, he much preferred Schumann's "The Happy Farmer," which I would play on the piano for him at bedtime as a way to get him to brush his teeth. Recently I played my nineteen-year-old Andy a recording of the Bach concerto and asked him if it did anything special for him. He looked up and said, "No, not particularly; it sounds like all the other stuff you play." Alas, Andy is not particularly interested in music (he has other talents). Jenny likes music much more and plays her flute regularly even though she was not conscientiously exposed to fine music every night when she was a fetus!

When discussing music's power to help us remember, I told Oliver the story of one of my students who taped my lectures, studied the tapes, and then could recite the lectures back to me verbatim as long as she put them to song. Oliver was intrigued by this story and ended up including it in *Musicophilia*.

Oliver's descriptions of the powers of music therapy were very moving, but I wondered at the time if he exaggerated. Four years later, however, I saw music therapy in action and wrote to him all about it.

August 9, 2011

Dear Oliver,

A happy story:

My 89-year-old dad lives three miles from me in an assisted care facility. Physically, he's OK, but he's deeply depressed and has lost all desire to get out of bed. My sadness and frustration over his condition is mitigated somewhat by the staff at the assisted care facility, who treat my father and the other residents with enormous dignity and compassion. I visit my dad three times per week, and every time I enter the facility, I feel like I have been absorbed into a cocoon of kindness. Sometimes, I think the staff people are the most deserving individuals on earth.

Yet, even the staff can't change my father. Often when I visit, he is lying in bed, curled into a fetal position. His left eye has crossed right into his nose. I sit him up and put on his glasses. As we engage in conversation, his eyes straighten. He looks at the art books I bring, keeps track of stories I tell him, and laughs at my jokes. But he only permits a certain amount of engagement. When I got him a good pair of hearing aids, he reacted violently—as if to say, "Don't force me into the world." I took the hearing aids back and wondered if I should just let my dad be. Still, it would be nice if he had moments of pleasure.

Every night, all through my childhood, my father played his violin. When my sister and I were too agitated to sleep, he would come into our shared bedroom and play us to sleep. During my mother's last decade, my father played for her every night, which calmed her Parkinson's tremors and allowed her to drift into sleep. In a sense, my father had been our family's music therapist. Perhaps I could find a music therapist for my dad.

After some research, I hired Rusty, a 40-ish-year-old man who reminds me of a large puppy. At the first music therapy session, Rusty bounced into my dad's room and began to play his guitar and sing. I sang along. My father lay on his back on his bed, unmoving. The only time he opened his eyes was to say good-bye to Rusty.

"Don't worry," Rusty said to me when he saw my sad face, "It can take some time for people to warm up to me." But how could anyone not warm up to Rusty immediately with his kind face and rich tenor voice?

The breakthrough came during the second music therapy session. "What should we sing?" Rusty asked, and I suggested Pete Seeger songs, since my parents used to take me and my siblings to Pete Seeger concerts when we were kids. But the songs had no effect on my dad. My father likes folk songs, but his real love is chamber music. So I started to hum the melody to Schubert's Trout Quintet, and Rusty improvised on his guitar. My father opened his eyes. Then Rusty moved into a syncopated version of "Ode to Joy." My dad applauded.

With each subsequent music therapy session, my father got more and more engaged. Before the fifth session, I came into my father's room and told him that Rusty would be coming soon. My father hoisted himself into a sitting position and asked for more room light. During the session, Rusty gave him a pair of mini-cymbals, which he beat in time to the music.

Last Friday, during the sixth music therapy session, several other residents peeked into my father's room. "Come in! Come in!" Rusty and I shouted, and the staff rushed to get additional chairs. Soon there were six other elderly residents in the room, singing and clapping. We sang World War II–era songs, even "Bei Mir Bist Du Schoen." Two women got up and danced, holding on to each other (otherwise they would have both fallen over). One of the residents caught my eye and pointed to my father. "He smiled," she said.

If I had not read your books, I never would have known about music therapy. Now I've witnessed its powers. Rusty comes every Friday afternoon. It's something to look forward to.

Love,

Stereo Sue

Music therapy became so popular with the residents in the assisted care facility that we moved the activity from my father's bedroom to a common area. Rusty, the staff, and I continued to be amazed by the residents' transformations. I wrote to Oliver again about them on October 21, 2011.

In the past, these residents hardly seemed like distinct individuals to me. Now, with the singing, their personalities come to the fore. Last week, one ancient woman (a former cellist and peace activist) asked if anyone knew the words to "Union Maid." I told her I knew them, so we sang the song together, harmonizing with each other.

Oliver was working furiously at that time on his upcoming book *Hallucinations*, but he took the time to send a short letter back to me two weeks later, writing,

Fascinated (and moved) by your account of responses to the music therapist—the patients <u>individuating</u> before your eyes.

Action, Perception, Cognition

Oliver's tales about music and my own studies of vision began to converge shortly after reading the draft of *Musicophilia*. For the next year we discussed how our senses, actions, and memory shape our understanding and knowledge of the world. There are many ways, for example, to recognize things in our surroundings, as Oliver brought out in his case histories. Dr. P. in *The Man Who Mistook His Wife for a Hat* had visual agnosia. He could recognize specific features of an object, such as its color and shape, but could not integrate the features to identify the object as a whole. Although he couldn't recognize a glove by sight, he could identify it in the act of putting it on. In *Musicophilia*, Oliver discussed the case of Rachel Y., who, after a brain injury, lost her sense of perfect pitch but could identify a pitch in the act of singing it. I wondered whether or not Dr. P.'s recognition of the glove and Rachel Y.'s identification of the note could be considered types of perception. I also thought that many people shared similar difficulties to Dr. P. and Rachel Y. in their ordinary experiences with music. So, in a February 22, 2007, email to Kate and Oliver, I wrote,

> I've been mulling around another thought regarding music, which comes from my reading about vision. A variety of

evidence indicates that we may have in essence two visual systems, one for perception and one for action. These two visual systems seem to follow two different neuronal pathways in the brain. Thus, Goodale and Milner* in their book *Sight Unseen* describe a patient, Dee, who suffered an injury to her perception pathway. She can no longer look at a coffee cup, recognize it as a coffee cup, and name it as a coffee cup. But she has no trouble reaching out for it and picking it up. She can position her fingers properly around the handle of the cup. So somewhere in her brain, she recognizes the coffee cup. I wonder if Dr. P. was the same way. He might not have recognized a glove, but if you had asked him to put it on, would he have known how to do it? If so, somewhere in his brain, at least in the action pathway, he knew that the glove was a glove.

I think the same is true for many people and music. If you ask the average person to sing "Happy Birthday," they can do that. If you give them the starting pitch, most people can mimic the starting pitch and sing the song from there. So somewhere in their brain they know the notes and the relationship of the pitches to each other. Yet, if you ask the average person, particularly someone without music or ear training, to write down the notes, they would be lost even if you gave them the starting note. They would have difficulty giving a symbolic representation to the notes. (This is something that frustrates me.) So there seems to be a divide between action, the ability to hum the pitches, and perception, the ability to recognize and name the pitches and their relationship to each other. Oliver writes about Lawrence Wechsler, who can hum a tune accurately but cannot say which pitch is higher or lower than the next. And Rachel Y.

---

* Melvyn A. Goodale and A. David Milner are two influential neuroscientists whose research suggests that our visual system comprises two pathways: one for perception (identification and recognition of objects) and one for action (manipulating objects).

writes that, after her injury, she remembers a pitch only because she remembers how it feels to sing it. She is depending upon her actions or memory of her actions, not her perception, to recognize the pitch. When I read this passage about Rachel Y., I wrote in the margin "Like Dee!" because Goodale and Milner's Dee rehabilitated herself in a similar way. She can recognize an object, e.g., a coffee cup, after she acts upon it. Without her perception pathway, she must use her own actions to recognize things.

Oliver was excited by this note and wrote a physical letter back to me that same day. As with my recent correspondence, he seemed to be thinking out loud, trying out ideas, as much for himself as for me.

While this morning, curiously (in another context—and thinking of blindsight) I quoted the case of "Dee" (and it may be relevant to Dr. P.—who could indeed act when he could not perceive—not just with the glove, but with dressing himself). I have been more inclined to put the matter in the more general terms of conscious/unconscious, explicit/ implicit, and (a phrase Gilbert Ryle used to use) "knowing what" and "knowing how." Also "facts" and "acts." Clive[*] does not know that he knows Bach—but give him the score, a first note, and he will play a Bach fugue. He does not know what he knows—but what he knows is not in the mode of "knowing that"; or "knowing what." Thus his knowledge can't be <u>used</u> (for anything else). . . . I think too (I am jumping) of how the blind John Hull,[†] some years after losing his sight, had so lost his visual <u>imagery</u> that he could not imagine a 3, say what it looked like—but he could

---

[*] Clive was a musician with severe amnesia whom Oliver wrote about in *Musicophilia*.

[†] John M. Hull (1935–2015), a professor of religious education at the University of Birmingham in Great Britain, wrote a moving memoir called *Touching the Rock: An Experience of Blindness*.

instantly draw a "3" in the air. How can he then draw a 3 in the air?

A few lines later, Oliver returned to my main thought and clarified it. Recognizing a coffee cup by the act of picking it up or recognizing a musical pitch by the act of singing it is not the same as perceiving the cup or the pitch directly.

> . . . your point especially has to do with reclaiming a (feeling
> of) perception from one's own actions. And yet I am not
> sure that this actually occurs. When Dr. P. says, "My God,
> it's a glove!" he may still be lacking the ability to perceive
> it. He will "know" that it is a glove, but by inference from
> his own actions, rather than by perceiving it as such. There
> is something similar with Clive and the Bach. . . . All of
> these examples emphasize the difference between action/
> automatism/unconsciousness/implicitness and perception/
> choice/consciousness/explicitness—and Goodale and Milner's
> special strength is to have demonstrated the distinctness
> of the two ways so well in their patient(s), and the fact
> that they can be dissociated, have their own quite distinct
> anatomical paths.

Oliver's discussion of contrasting kinds of knowledge reminded me of another dichotomy, one he had mentioned in his first letter to me as well as in "Stereo Sue." This was the difference between (as Bertrand Russell dubbed it) "knowledge by description" (i.e., facts) and "knowledge by acquaintance" (i.e., experience). Thus, my understanding of the mechanisms behind stereopsis (knowledge by description) could not substitute for my experience of first seeing with stereopsis (knowledge by acquaintance). All this brought to mind a story I had read in

The New Yorker, which I described in my next letter to Oliver, dated March 27, 2007.

> I read an article in *The New Yorker* about a year ago (Feb. 27, 2006, pp. 27–28) about a man named Doug Bruce, who suffered from total retrograde amnesia. His amnesia was different from Clive's in that he has no memory whatsoever of anything in his past and did not know who he was. However, he can set down new memories. . . . The story about Doug Bruce was written in an optimistic light because Doug describes his joy in experiencing things "for the first time." In particular, he writes, "Since the accident, I feel a childlike—or what I imagine to be a childlike—wonder at new experiences, but also an analytical understanding. . . . When I first held snow, it was about both the feeling of the crystals in my hand and my understanding of the molecular structure. . . . And I feel very privileged to have experienced, as an adult, falling in love for the first time, the way a teen-ager probably would."
>
> I loved these quotes and cut out the article and kept it in my coat pocket for several months. Although (thankfully) I did not go through the tragic experiences that Doug Bruce did, I know a little about what it is like to have both an analytical understanding of something, e.g., stereopsis, and yet to experience a childlike wonder when seeing in stereo depth for the first time. (I like very much the way you describe this in "Stereo Sue.") Coincidentally, some of Doug Bruce's and my compelling first impressions were of snow.

One year later, while on vacation in the Yucatán, I became greatly excited by reading Geerat Vermeij's memoir *Privileged Hands*. Oliver had taught me that we can learn a lot about how we come to understand the world through people who, because of sensory loss, experience it differently. I was fascinated by Vermeij, who has made important contributions to our understanding of evolution and has constructed an evolutionary history of mollusks, despite the fact that he is blind. On February 9, 2008, I wrote to Oliver all about him and his book.

> I used to think that a blind person would lack a good sense of geometry or of three dimensions, but this is clearly not the case. I was very struck by Vermeij's description of Braille and his use of a slate and stylus. He points out that listening to books on tape is a passive experience while reading Braille is active. After one writes Braille by punching the dots through the paper, one has to turn the paper over to read it. Thus, each letter must be written in mirror image fashion! He claims that this process quickly becomes second nature. No wonder he could recapture the geometry of molluscan shells by handling them and turning them over in his hands.

Oliver was indeed familiar with Geerat Vermeij and, in his reply on February 19, 2008, compared Vermeij to a blind geometer who "felt" and then figured out the requisite topology to show how a sphere could be turned inside out. He was also struck by Vermeij's conclusion that reading Braille was an active process in contrast to listening to audiobooks, which was more passive.

> Apropos of listening to books vs. Braille there is a fascinating story and insight here with regard to Helen Keller, who (as you probably know) was accused of "plagiarism" when she was 11 or 12, because a short story she wrote turned out to be identical in theme, and sometimes in language, with a story for children published a few years before. She herself said she had no memory of ever having heard the story, and thought it was her own invention. In her autobiography

she says that if something was read to her, and "passively received," she might subsequently be uncertain of its source, whether internal or external. If she read by Braille, "actively," there was never any ambiguity or doubt.

In his memoir, Vermeij described how hard it was to convince educators and scientists that he could learn and contribute as well as a sighted person. This reminded me of a story about one of my students whom I described to Oliver.

Katie was profoundly deaf since birth but decided to live in a hearing world. She learned to lip-read and speak. In class, she would sit in the front row, her gaze fixated on my mouth (which I found a bit disconcerting.) As a hearing person, I doubt that I will ever appreciate the enormous effort and focus that went into her typical school day.

Naturally, Katie was interested in the subject of hearing, so one of my colleagues and I took Katie on a trip to the Massachusetts Eye and Ear Infirmary. There, we met a very learned auditory scientist, who gave us a tour of the hearing laboratories. It was a wonderful day, but shortly before we left, we all sat down for a casual chat. The scientist asked Katie what she planned to do upon graduation, and Katie said that she hoped to go to medical school and become a psychiatrist.

"Oh no," said the scientist, "you can't do that. You can't hear (as if Katie didn't know this!). You can't pick up the nuances and subtleties in your patient's speech. You'll have to choose another profession."

Katie seemed to take this pronouncement in stride. Shortly afterward, we thanked the scientist for a fascinating day, left the laboratory, and emerged onto the street. As I watched Katie bravely move into the traffic to hail a taxicab, all my maternal instincts came to the fore. As we settled into the cab, I said to her, "That scientist may know a lot about hearing, but he knows nothing about you. If you want to be a psychiatrist, become a psychiatrist. You may not hear people's speech, but you pick up on nonverbal cues that hearing people are not aware of. Moreover, you will be an inspiration to your patients. . . ."

I would have gone on in this vein, but Katie stopped me with a mischievous smile.

"Don't worry, Sue," she said, "You have forgotten. I have been not listening to people for my whole life!"

Oliver was clearly moved by this story.

I am very glad you were so affirmative with your deaf student after meeting the stupid psychiatrist[*]—there are totally deaf psychiatrists, and patients, who can enjoy the fullest interactions (there is a paper about this by Arlow,[†] the first reference in the biblio of SEEING VOICES)—and one blinded psychiatrist whom I mention in THE MIND'S EYE— now a rabbi too (Dennis Shulman) felt that his sensitivities to subtle expressions were <u>increased</u> by his blindness.

I closed my own letter by returning to my encounters in the Yucatán.

This letter will end, as it began, on a molluscan theme. Between the Mayan ruins and the mangroves, there was much to see in the Yucatán. However, my favorite sight of

---

[*] Oliver meant the scientist who told Katie that she couldn't be a psychiatrist.
[†] Jacob A. Arlow (1912–2004) was an influential American psychiatrist and psychoanalyst.

the vacation was unplanned. I was snorkeling one day in a very pretty reef when I had my first encounter with wild squid. I am used to seeing these creatures in the holding tanks at the MBL in Woods Hole. There they seem dull and white. As a result, when I first saw these colorful swimmers while snorkeling, it took me a moment to realize that I was not looking at another type of fish. There were four squid, ranging from about eight inches to a foot in length, swimming in parallel formation. Their body displays continually changed from horizontal tiger stripes on a red-brown mantle to vertical stripes and polka dots that were colored blue-green and green-yellow. I watched them for a long time but have no idea what they were saying to each other. Maybe, you could have figured it out.

Malacologically yours,

Stereo Sue

Malacology is the study of mollusks, and squid are a type of mollusk. Oliver ended his letter in kind with a more creative and very Oliver-ish sign-off:

My own first experience of squids in the wild was very much like yours; a little vertical squadron of them—and I felt (probably a delusion) that they were as curious about me as I was about them.

So, teuthophilically* yours,

monour an Oliy

---

* Teuthis means squid, and "teuthophilically" is an Oliver creation meaning lover of squid.

Tungsten Birthday

On July 2, 2007, I received the following email from Kate:

> Oliver's tungstenth birthday approacheth! (If you are anywhere near NYC on July 9th, we'd love to have you join us for sushi dinner with a few friends.)

Oliver's first and abiding love had been for the elements and the periodic table. That's why, during his visit to my home, he had been charmed when my son Andy sang him Tom Lehrer's "The Elements" song. Oliver even equated people's ages with the atomic number of elements. Since he was turning seventy-four, his element this year was tungsten. So I bought him a tungsten top for his birthday gift and boarded the train for New York City for his July 9 party. Finding his home apartment was easy, since it was near the building with his office. At the party I met other neurologists, a music therapist, mineral lovers, an expert on ferns, and an artist-photographer of wetland birds. The latter, Rosalie Winard,* was a good friend of Temple

---

* Rosalie Winard's stunning and moving photographs of wetland birds can be seen in her book *Wild Birds of the American Wetlands*.

Grandin* and introduced Oliver to Temple. After our initial meeting, Rosalie and I became good friends, and she generously shot
some of the photos of me and Oliver that appear in this book. All
the rooms in Oliver's apartment, including the kitchen, were lined
with bookshelves displaying cards identifying the books' subjects and
leaving no doubt that Oliver was an eclectic reader. At the party,
Oliver showed me a red/green anaglyph he had made as a boy of his
London neighborhood, as well as another of cacti, but he could no
longer see the depth in them as well as I could.

---

* Temple Grandin is a professor of Animal Science at Colorado State University and has
  written books on both autism and animal behavior, including *Thinking in Pictures*, *Animals
  Make Us Human*, and *Visual Thinking*. Oliver wrote about her and her autism in *An
  Anthropologist on Mars*.

In Juxtaposition

In late September 2007, I again traveled to Manhattan, this time to visit my new friend Rosalie Winard, whom I first met at Oliver's birthday party. During my New York stay, we spent an evening with Oliver at his apartment enjoying a sushi dinner (one of Oliver's favorite meals) topped off with chocolates from Li-Lac, a chocolate shop down the street. While we chatted, I told Oliver that I read his book *Migraine* while having a migraine. Since my head was throbbing, I put a bag of frozen blueberries on it to quell the pain. The blueberries started to melt, staining the book blue, which seemed a good reflection of the book's subject. Oliver then told me that he liked to read books in the bath. While reading Brian Greene's book *The Elegant Universe*, it slipped from his hands into the water. Sometime later, he met Greene and had him autograph his waterlogged copy!

Knowing that both Rosalie and I loved to swim, Oliver invited us to swim with him and a friend the next morning at an indoor pool at Chelsea Piers. His friend was Lynne Cox, one of the greatest long-distance swimmers ever, who had recently written a book called *Swimming to Antarctica*. In my thank-you letter to Oliver, sent one week later, I wrote, "I felt a little sheepish swimming with Lynne—it's a bit like playing piano four hands with Emanuel Ax. But Lynne could not have been friendlier or more down-to-earth."

At the time of the visit, Oliver had finished *Musicophilia* and was turning his attention from music and the brain to vision and hallucinations. Three months earlier, because of the tumor in his right eye and the resulting visual distortions, the central region of his right retina had been lasered. If Oliver closed his good left eye and looked only with his right, he saw a huge black opacity in the center of his gaze. As he walked, he saw with his right eye alone only the lower half of people. And without central vision in his right eye, he lost most of his stereovision, so our conversation turned to our shared experiences of what it was like to be stereoblind. I mentioned, for example, that all objects framed by a window used to look in the same plane as the window glass. "Yes, yes!" Oliver answered and told us that he recently saw his piano teacher sitting against a window and thought the tree branches outside the window were coming out of her head! After dinner, we went up to the roof of his apartment building, a pleasant space with chairs and plants. Oliver, now lacking stereovision, proceeded very cautiously on the stairs. While on the roof, I looked down only briefly at Eighth Avenue many stories below and explained that my stereopsis, which gave me a much greater sense of the volumes of space, had also given me a fear of heights. Oliver nodded: With the loss of vision in one eye, he was now indifferent to heights. "Seeing with one eye," Oliver concluded, and I agreed, "produces a different concept of space."

Shortly afterward, a package from Oliver appeared in my mailbox along with a letter.

OLIVER SACKS, M.D.   10/10/07

2 HORATIO ST. #3G · NEW YORK, NY · 10014
TEL: 212.633.8373 · FAX: 212.633.8928
MAIL@OLIVERSACKS.COM

Dear Sue,

   I very much enjoyed seeing
you again - and yr letter. It
is intriguing to get more details of
the concept-of-space parts which you
sounded (and I am now exploring
in Nurse). I saw another chap,
yesterday, who had lost central vision
in one eye (from melanoma), and he
too commented on a variety of unexpected
(+ sometimes comic) difficulties —
especially c measuring, pouring etc. when
cooking in the kitchen - And my analyst
this morning told me of a seamstress

OLIVER SACKS, M.D.

2 HORATIO ST. #3G · NEW YORK, NY · 10014
TEL: 212.633.8373 · FAX: 212.633.8928
MAIL@OLIVERSACKS.COM

...he man who became completely unable to thread a needle + sew on a button when she lost an eye --

On the subject of STEREO I enclose Valyus' grand book, which was a great source of pleasure + information to me once (along w. its many-many stereo-illustrations) - but I think now that it would be of more use to you — and more fun — than it is for me. So I hope you find it (or least in part) useful and/or enjoyable —

let's keep in touch — and let me know how yr book is going —

Best.
Oliver

OLIVER SACKS, M.D.   10/10/07
2 HORATIO ST. #3G · NEW YORK, NY · 10014
TEL: 212.633.8373 · FAX: 212.633.8928
MAIL@OLIVERSACKS.COM

Dear Sue,

I <u>very</u> much enjoyed seeing you again—<u>and</u> your letter. It is
intriguing to get more details of the concept-of-space path
which you ascended (and I am now exploring in reverse).
I saw another chap, yesterday, who had lost central vision
in one eye (from melanoma), and he too commented on a
variety of unexpected (and sometimes comic) difficulties—
especially with measuring, pouring etc. when cooking in
the kitchen. And my analyst* this morning told me of a
seamstress he met who became completely unable to thread
a needle and sew on a button when she lost an eye.

On the subject of STEREO I enclose Valyus' grand book,
which was a great source of pleasure and information to me
once (along with its many, many stereo-illustrations)—but I
think now that it would be of more use to you—and more
fun—than it is for me. So I hope you find it (at least in part)
useful and/or enjoyable.

Let's keep in touch—and let me know how your book is
going.

Best,

Oliver

---

* As Oliver described in his memoir *On the Move*, he began seeing a psychoanalyst, Dr.
Leonard Shengold, in 1966, and continued to consult him regularly until shortly before
Oliver died.

The book was *Stereoscopy* by N. A. Valyus, published in 1986. On the inside cover, Oliver had written an inscription:

For Stereo-Sue,

from ex-stereo-Oliver,

with admiration
^ warmest good wishes

"For Stereo-Sue, from ex-stereo-Oliver, with admiration and warmest good wishes." By this time, I had collected lots of books on binocular vision and stereoscopy, including classics such as *Researches in Binocular Vision* by Kenneth Ogle and *Foundations of Cyclopean Perception* by Bela Julesz, but I had not even heard of Valyus or his book.

I learned that Nikolai Adamovich Valyus was born in 1909 and was a professor and scientist in Moscow who designed instruments for, among other uses, stereoscopic cinematography. His book was full of anaglyphs and stereo pairs and information on the physiology of binocular vision, stereoscopic devices, and the uses of stereoscopy in science and art. He was an expert on all things stereo in the former USSR but was less well known to most western scientists—except Oliver.

Reading Oliver's letter ("I enclose Valyus' grand book, which was a great source of pleasure and information to me once—but I think now that it would be of more use to you") left me feeling very sad. Was there anything positive I could say about seeing without stereopsis that might make him feel better? So in my next letter (October 21, 2007, now double-spaced and printed in 18-point font), I told him of a little incident that happened to me three decades earlier.

When I was 22 years old, I went to visit my brother in Paris. One morning, he and I bought some croissants and stopped at a garden to enjoy our breakfast. As we were eating, I became fascinated by a sprinkler that was rotating in a wide circle, drenching all the plants within its reach. At first the sprinkler appeared to me to be rotating clockwise, then counterclockwise, then clockwise again. I kept exclaiming, "It changed direction; there it goes again; it did it again!" My brother studied the sprinkler but saw it turn in only one direction. Presumably, his stereopsis left no ambiguity as to when the sprinkler was coming toward or receding from him.

Recently, I emailed my brother to see if he could recall the incident. His reply indicated that he, too, remembered that happy morning quite vividly. He wrote back,

"Oh yea—it was the Jardin des Plantes in the 5th arrondissement—a combination science museum and garden. As I remember we were standing in an arcade looking into a courtyard of trained fruit trees being watered, giggling about your trick of rotating the sprinklers at the touch of a brain wave."

I used to play with reversible figures such as Necker cubes[*] all the time and could switch from one percept to the other very quickly. I even thought that I was particularly good at this. Perhaps, my brain could generate rapid perceptual changes because it dealt with more ambiguity in the third dimension. If so, perhaps, you can get very good at reversible figures. It doesn't make up for your visual losses, but it might provide some entertainment.

Much of our correspondence in 2007 through 2009 involved discussions about music and *Musicophilia*, progress reports on my own first book, Oliver's reaction to a close-to-final draft, and discussions

---

[*] A Necker cube can be seen in two ways:

of our poor navigational skills and my compass hat (see page 137). Yet, the theme of stereopsis and our changing concepts of space continually resurfaced. On February 9, 2008, I wrote,

> I have been thinking a great deal about one's sense of distance and space because it is these concepts that are changing most for me now. . . . This sense of distance keeps changing and expanding. Everything is considerably more spread out; my bedroom is less cluttered, an airport less crowded, and a forest contains layers upon layers of trees.
>
> Today, I was driving along a flat straight road lined on both sides by stores and strip malls. This is the kind of visually complicated environment that used to unnerve me. But, while I was stopped at a light, I could see, perhaps one quarter mile down the road, a second set of lights and beyond them a third set. I could see that all the lights were red and, considerably past the lights, the mountains stretched out toward the horizon. This was incredible. I have never taken in so much space before. The world, prior to my gaining binocularity, was not so much flat as contracted. Space was collapsed.
>
> I wonder what it is like for you. I worry that your sense of space has contracted. Does your prior stereo experience allow you to still see the landscape as stretching a great distance toward the horizon? Do you still have that sense of palpable space between objects? I hope the scotoma is less troublesome (and not getting any bigger) and that you are more confident when walking down stairs.

In his letter of February 19, 2008, Oliver replied,

> You put it very well when you speak of space as "contracted," even "collapsed," in the absence of binocular vision. I

continually find this so—find that near objects and far not only
have no space between them, but are repeatedly juxtaposed,
absurdly, on the same "plane," despite manifest incongruities
of size and character. (Yesterday, at my analyst, I saw a little
pile of colored sticky labels apparently sitting on top of my
water bottle—while knowing this was not the case, I could
not voluntarily alter the perception. I have not yet developed
sufficient in the way of head-moving automatisms to
disambiguate things like this.) When I was in London I met, and
have since received a fascinating article from a young musician
who suddenly lost all hearing in one ear—for him too space has
"collapsed," at least musical space, and aural space—he describes
this with more depth and detail than the Norwegian surgeon I
describe in my book. I find it difficult to separate "percept" from
"concept" here. I really think the idea of space (but what does one
mean by this?) can collapse. And I am not sure, although they are
normally correlated, about the connections of visual space, aural
space, kinesthetic or motor space, etc.

. . .

Everything you describe about space expanding,
extending, is now in reverse for me. The only
"compensation"—a small one because I am not a visual
artist, and cannot make use of it—is that everything being
flattened and juxtaposed, I have a stronger sense of "visual
composition," of seeing (sometimes beautiful) still-lives.

Oliver recognized from the very start that my achievement of
stereovision provided me with a novel perception of space, a "quale,"
or sensation that I could not previously have imagined. Indeed,
when he first visited me back in 2005 and saw my delight at viewing stereograms, he rubbed his beard and mused aloud to Bob and
Ralph, "It's like she's developed a whole new sense." For my first

forty-eight years, I had not combined or fused the images from my two eyes. Perhaps, then, it is not surprising that learning this skill led to a whole new perceptual experience. For Oliver's first seventy-three years, however, he had seen with stereopsis. With almost every glance, he had perceived space as (to use his words) a "wonderful, transparent medium" and "a hospitable, deep realm in which I could locate myself and wander at will." So, on June 1, 2009, I wrote,

Dear Oliver,

. . .

It surprises me that you have experienced such a severe flattening of your visual world and a compressed concept of space. Before I gained stereopsis, I did not think of space as (to use your words) "voluminous, as providing a medium, a place, a habitation for solid objects," but I had no prior experience to create such a concept. You, on the other hand, had seventy-three years in which you relished your stereopsis, and I thought these experiences would help fill in what you were now missing.

Oliver responded on June 15, noting our parallel experiences of stereoblindness, including the view of our reflection in a mirror and a diminished fear of heights.

Yes, it surprised me that (despite 73 years of stereopsis, even hyperstereopsis) I now confront such a flattened world, and one where, in the absence of other cues, I find it difficult to give any meaning to comparative terms like "near" and "far," closer and more distant, even foreground and background. I "function" reasonably well, after a fashion can drive competently and confidently, at least in daylight (night-driving I try to avoid, because in the absence of visual surround I cannot tell how far away lights are)—but the quale of depth is quite gone (at least when I look—it is there, for what it's worth, where I have a crescent of peripheral vision[*]). Many of my experiences are the exact opposite of what you experience now—you write, beautifully, about the delight of seeing your figure advance and recede in the mirror. I try to wipe a spot off my suit, and find the spot is on the mirror, my image is on the mirror—there is absolutely no sense anymore of my reflection being behind the mirror, no more "through the looking-glass." You speak of the sudden shock/fear/awe/ vertigo etc looking down from a great height, or a precipice, in Hawaii.[†] I used to have quite severe acrophobia, with all sorts of autonomic reactions and imaginations of falling from heights—now I am almost dangerously indifferent to them.

It intrigues me that you now find that 2D representations of space—paintings, movies etc—so evocative of volume, space (as they should be). I find them much less evocative. It is as if you have gained a new sense of space, and I have lost one. I find motion parallax[‡] indispensable, but it gives me no quale of stereopsis.

. . .

I have been reading J. J. Gibson (THE PERCEPTION OF THE VISUAL WORLD, THE SENSES AS PERCEPTUAL SYSTEMS)—have you read him? He is marvelous, and was perhaps the first to emphasize that one can hardly speak of perception without action, interaction—of seeing without

---

[*] At this point, Oliver retained some noncentral vision in his right eye, which could be combined with input from his left eye to provide some peripheral stereopsis.

[†] This fear arose after I gained stereopsis.

[‡] When we move side to side, objects close to us appear to move faster in our visual field than objects farther away, and this relative motion or motion parallax provides a sense of depth order—what's in front and what's behind. I, too, had always used motion parallax to infer depth order, but only after I gained stereopsis did motion parallax provide me with a sense of the pockets of space between objects.

speaking of looking, of hearing without listening, of smelling without sniffing etc—an "ecological" view. (I think Dale Purves has somewhat similar thoughts—as well as "extended consciousness" philosophers like Alva Noë.) Gibson himself downplays stereo—as Purves does—sees it as just one way, one of several, of getting information about a 3D world—but I think these quantitative or behavioural measures, which are nothing to do with the quale, miss the point—and that it needs, not behavioural tests, but descriptions of individual experiences (like yours and mine) as well.

When I first began to see in 3D, I was so overwhelmed and over-joyed by my new views that I wondered if I was going crazy. It is a sad irony that this man, who immediately grasped just how miracu-lous my new stereovision was to me, should lose his. Two years later, when Oliver was writing *The Mind's Eye*, a book that contained five case histories, including his story and mine, he wrote to me, "So your story, and my story, will be in direct juxtaposition."

Outed

On March 19, 2008, I visited Oliver again in New York with our friend Rosalie. Oliver, who had been keeping diaries since the age of fourteen, showed us his "melanoma journal." He seemed very subdued. During that season, Oliver and I also exchanged several letters and, in all of them, he commented that he was feeling low and distracted. His major push to finish *Musicophilia* was over; he was writing about Darwin and flowering plants ("Darwin and the Meaning of Flowers") and was planning a "visual" book. In doing so, he was forced to revisit his visual losses.

Two months later, on May 30, 2008, Oliver was scheduled to give a live interview with the science journalist Robert Krulwich at the World Science Festival at the Metropolitan Museum of Art. "Stereo (yours and mine as a start) will certainly be one of the visual subjects which Robert and I will chat about at the Met on Friday—hope you can make it!" Oliver wrote. On the morning of the talk, as I rode down the highway to New York City and the festival, my cell phone rang. It was Robert on the line. He would be interviewing Oliver during the festival and planned to talk about Oliver's eye tumor, his distorted vision, and loss of stereovision. He was even going to show pictures from Oliver's journal. But, that morning, Oliver had called to say he didn't want to talk about his vision. Robert resisted, telling

Oliver in no uncertain terms, "Dr. Sacks, the train has left the station." So, now, Robert wondered if I could come up onstage for part
of the talk so to take the attention off Oliver. I agreed, and Robert
instructed me to introduce myself to the usher when I got to the Met
auditorium. They would put me in a seat at a particular part of the
auditorium, and at some point, Robert would call for me.

When I arrived in New York City, I first went to Rosalie's apartment. She insisted that if I was going up onstage, I needed more
stylish clothing and so dressed me for the evening. At the Met, I
gave the usher my name and was directed to a seat near the aisle
on the left-hand side, facing the stage. Robert and Oliver came out
onto the stage and sat opposite each other with a large plant on the
table between them. They began talking about vision, and Robert
projected pictures that Oliver drew of his bedroom ceiling fan as seen
with his right eye. Some of the fan blades were missing; they were not
seen because of damage to his right retina. They talked about stereovision, and Oliver added, somewhat wistfully, that he wished Stereo
Sue was present so she could describe what it was like to gain, rather
than lose, stereovision. To which, Robert responded, "She's here, in
the audience!" Oliver feigned surprise, "She is?!" Robert called me
up, and I got out of my seat and walked through the crowd of seven
hundred to the stage. There was a seat for me, opposite Robert, and
next to and to the right of Oliver. As I sat down, Robert casually
pulled a hand-held microphone out of the large leafy plant. (He and
Oliver wore smaller mikes.) Then Robert asked me about gaining
stereovision and I said: "I can see how the outer branches of a tree
enclose and capture whole volumes of space through which the inner
branches penetrate. . . . I still find it breathtaking; it still takes me by
surprise; my new vision fills me with childlike wonder." Out of the
corner of my eye, I saw Oliver nod. Then I returned to my seat while
Robert and Oliver continued the conversation.

After the event, I went up to the stage to find Oliver. He had been asking for me, but when I saw him, he was quiet. As we walked through the museum's Egyptian displays and paused at a sarcophagus, Oliver mentioned that he had been "outed," meaning that he had spoken in public about his vision losses. He seemed very sad, and I didn't know how to comfort him. I also wondered about his use of the term, "outed." I assumed he was gay and wondered if that was another secret he held close.

Like Oliver, I brought my personal story to the public and, as a result, felt exposed. Every time I talked about my crossed eyes, I relived the shame and humiliation I felt as a child. So I think I understood Oliver's ambivalence about telling a personal story in public. After my surgeries, most people didn't notice my crossed eyes. But Oliver detected my strabismus even before I mentioned it to him at our very first meeting at Dan's launch party in 1996. My secret was out with him from the start, and, in the end, he enabled me to use it to help others.

Musical Interlude II

On November 6, 2008, I wrote Oliver a thank you note for writing the foreword to *Fixing My Gaze* and also for his earlier comments on the book in his October 13 letter. This could not have been easy for him, since he was losing the very stereovision that I had gained. I knew he was feeling low in part because he was now writing about his visual losses. So, I enclosed a gift. I wanted to find something that took his mind off the visual, and a book I recently read provided the solution.

Dear Oliver,

Thanks so much for writing the foreword to my book. It emphasizes all the important themes in such a lyrical way, and I hope the book lives up to the foreword's stunning last paragraph. Given your visual losses, it must have been difficult to read a book about the wonders of stereovision, and I very much appreciate your willingness to do this. Thanks also for your letter of October 13 and all the positive comments about my book. It gives me more confidence as the book goes to publication.

I have enclosed a small gift, the book *Violin Dreams* by Arnold Steinhardt, who is the first violinist of the Guarneri

String Quartet. I read this book a week ago and fell in love with it. It is an "ode to the fascination and wonder of" music and the violin and a wonderful history of violinists and violin making. One recurrent theme is built around Bach's Chaconne (fifth movement of the D minor partita) and another around Steinhardt's rich dream life. I was moved by his description of the pianist Arthur Loesser dancing to Bach's D minor partita. (I know you are not fond of dancing, but give this a try. I danced to it myself, and this opened up a different way to hear the music.)

. . .

In *Violin Dreams*, Steinhardt writes over and over again about Bach's Chaconne. This shouldn't have surprised me given the piece's power, a power you also described in *Musicophilia* when you wrote about a young violinist playing the Chaconne at the tip of Manhattan during an anniversary for 9/11. Often, the Chaconne's opening chords play in my head and remind me of my talented but complicated father.

The book includes a CD of the D minor partita so I have also enclosed the sheet music for the piece. That way, you can see and hear the musical structure and landscape at the same time. I hope the notes on the score are not too small for you to read.

Since this letter is on a musical theme, I thought I'd close by telling you about Fred, my piano tuner, a very curious character. Fred moves like a robot and speaks in an absolute monotone, emphasizing every consonant, and giving each syllable equal weight. On his first visit, he walked up to the piano, looked carefully at all the music I was playing, studied the family photos displayed around the room, and then sat at the piano to play. To my surprise, he played a piece that was romantic and complex, perhaps something by Chopin, and he played with a fluidity and grace that was completely lacking in his speech and other movements. Then he began to tune, first using his tuning fork to adjust the strings for the A 440 key[*] and tuning all the other keys by listening for the beats among the intervals. *What an odd duck*, I thought. *I hope he tunes pianos better than he interacts with or understands people.*

After his tuning, the piano sounded wonderful, and I found myself playing it more and more. Since that first visit, Fred has returned every six months to take care of the piano. One day, however, he arrived with an assistant. He asked if the assistant could tune the piano for him. Since Fred looked flustered and distracted, I readily agreed. A week later, Fred called to ask me how the piano sounded. I told him that I thought the pitch was OK, but something was different—the piano sounded too percussive. Fred said he'd be back in six months for a retuning.

Fred returned six months later, retuned the piano, and once again called me about a week later to ask me about the piano. "It's back to its old self," I told him happily and asked him what he had done. Fred told me that he voiced the keys. On his next visit, I asked him what he meant by voicing the keys, and he showed me how he adjusted the felt that was hit by the hammers connected to each key. "You like a mellow sound to your piano," he said (in his monotone), "so I have to voice the keys accordingly." I was really surprised and asked him how he knew what I liked. (*I* didn't know what I liked.) "Oh," he said, "I know what you like by talking with you, seeing what you play, and observing the particular wear and tear you give the piano." Then, he added, "I have to

---

[*] A 440 refers to the pitch whose frequency is 440 Hz and, on the piano, is the A above middle C.

know what a person is like, before I can tune their piano."

Yours in tune,

Sue

OLIVER SACKS, M.D.
2 HORATIO ST. #3G · NEW YORK, NY · 10014
TEL: 212.633.8373 · FAX: 212.633.8928
MAIL@OLIVERSACKS.COM

Nov 10, 08

Dear Sue,

What a lovely letter (as always)—and this time, book and CD too. I had heard of the book when it came out a couple of years ago—and now, thanks to you, I have started on it (just read the first chapter, so far—I have become a rather slow reader); <u>and</u> with the CD on my bedside CD-player, I have been playing and comparing Steinhardt's 1966 and 2006 versions of the D minor Partita (the earlier one is full of youthful energy and brilliance; but the later one, it seems to me, is far deeper and more reflective—and it is enormously helpful, thanks for this too, to have the score to hand).

The first time I ever saw a great violinist in the flesh was (I think) in 1943—tho' it could have been 1945 or so—when Yehudi Menuhin came to war-battered London, and played the Chaconne (this went through my mind when I heard it played, at the tip of Manhattan, on the anniversary of 9/11).

I was intrigued by your story of the monotonic and somewhat Asperger-sounding piano-tuner who then showed such sensitivity to <u>your</u> (musical) sensibilities. It makes me wonder (again!) whether, in various states, including autism, one can have a full response to music and musical emotion, in contrast to great emotional impoverishment in other spheres. One wonders whether this was true, in part, of Glenn Gould—and I like <u>his</u> later version (of the <u>Goldberg Variations</u>) much more than his earlier one.

Continuing on Bach—but at a much, much, much humbler level!—my piano teacher had four of her pupils at her apartment last week, playing pieces they were working on (for me, the E major Prelude in Book I of the 48, and a C minor Prelude in the Little Preludes and Fugues). It was the first time I had played for an audience (albeit a very tiny and forbearing audience) since the Mazurkas,* sixty-plus years ago.

I am very glad (and relieved!) you like the Foreword to your book—and, yes, having to think on stereo-vision did produce some pangs of nostalgia. I now have to face writing, at some length, about my own stereo-blindness, and its impact, as well as other visual symptoms (the one which strikes me most, now, is palinopsia,† though my visual field is full of little crawling hallucinations which I ignore). I am just getting back to my essay on Charles Bonnet syndrome‡— the draft "abandoned" in Sept '07.

Again, thanks! And the very best to you AND the book!

---

* Oliver is referring here to Chopin's Mazurkas, short piano pieces based on Polish dances and folk music. As a boy, Oliver memorized all fifty-nine of them. When he traveled with his parents to Switzerland shortly after the end of World War II, he played them at an impromptu concert at a Swiss hotel.

† Palinopsia occurs when you continue to see an image even after you've stopped looking at it.

‡ People who experience hallucinations following severe vision loss suffer from Charles Bonnet syndrome.

The Compass Hat

On May 13, 2009, Kate Edgar forwarded me an email from a gentleman with strabismus who was looking for advice. I replied by writing,

> Sure, Kate, I'll answer this man's email. There are some good optometrists in his area.
>
> I just got home from the Vision Sciences Society meeting. In my absence, Dan made me a fantastic Mother's Day present. It is a hat that he outfitted with a compass and circuitry so that it vibrates every time I turn my head north. I have a pathetic sense of direction, so maybe this will help. I'm off to take a walk around the neighborhood and check it out.

Then I signed off by writing, "No longer lost in South Hadley." Kate wrote back one minute later,

> Let me know how that works out; we might have to order one for Oliver!

Oliver and I each had a poor sense of direction, which was both frustrating and embarrassing. We always got lost. So, to help me, my husband Dan took an old floppy sun hat and embedded in it a compass and circuitry (see insert photo 9). When the compass registered north, the circuitry turned on a little motor causing the hat to buzz every time I turned my head to the north. I loved the hat. Could I use it to gain a sense of direction? Could the hat be a tool for "navigation therapy," like the Brock string had been a tool for vision therapy? In midlife, I had learned to see the world in 3D. With the hat, could I learn yet another new way of experiencing the world? Oliver was thinking along the same lines, which led to the following exchange.

OLIVER SACKS, M.D.

2 HORATIO ST. #3G · NEW YORK, NY · 10014
TEL: 212.633.8373 · FAX: 212.633.8928
MAIL@OLIVERSACKS.COM

May 18, 09

Dear Sue,

I am intrigued by your compass-hat, and look forward to hearing how much it can help you form internal maps, local and otherwise. I am intrigued because I am almost topagnosic myself—don't recognize places, no sense of direction, always getting lost, etc.—and had <u>also</u> wondered whether one might develop an extra, if artificial, magnetic sense.

A friend gave me some compass cufflinks years ago— and then I started carrying really powerful, large rare-earth magnets in my pockets—they try to align themselves with the earth's magnetic field. I wondered about inserting such magnets in one's ears, or one's spectacles, but you need more than their own (relatively feeble) pull—you need a <u>signal</u>, which is what Dan's hat provides. If we can't have magnetite granules* in our brains maybe magnetic hats can compensate.

. . .

What my compass hat provided, but Oliver's cufflinks did not, was—as he had written—a signal. The hat buzzed when I turned my head north. Its buzzing followed an action I had made. The coupling of our own movement with a sensation generally provides a powerful cue for learning so that Oliver and I wondered if this signal could help improve my sense of direction.

My lengthy response (considerably abridged here) was dated May 27, 2009.

Dear Oliver,

. . .

In the last few weeks, I've become obsessed with the directional sense and have asked lots of people, both strangers and friends, if they can tell me where north is. I can check their answers with my new hat. I've decided that people fall into one of three categories that I've named, the NATURALS, the BOY SCOUTS, and the CLUELESS.

The NATURALS are very well-oriented people who know where north is automatically. As they move about, they continually update their position on Earth with reference to external cues, although they are not usually aware that they are doing so.

---

* Magnetite granules are made of iron oxide and align with Earth's magnetic field.

The BOY SCOUTS can also tell where north is by using external cues, but they have to stop and think about it. The most commonly used cues are major roadways, large landmarks like mountains or rivers, and, of course, the sun. Some people take a sophisticated approach to using the sun as their compass by taking into account not only the time of day but also the month of the year and the tilt of the earth.

The name CLUELESS for the third group is both humorous and literal. CLUELESS people are unaware of where they are with respect to north and south. They don't pay attention to large external cues at all and are usually lost. (I just received your letter and realize that the neurological term is topagnosic.) Most people in this group will readily admit their cluelessness. I fall into the CLUELESS group. Although I usually have a good idea of how much time it will take to get from place to place, I don't see the geographical connection between different places. It feels like I am "beamed up" from one place to another just like the characters in *Star Trek*.

This lack of a geographical mental map contributes to a very bad memory of different places. Dan and I met as graduate students at Princeton in the mid-1970s. Although I was at Princeton for four and a half years and in my twenties at the time, I have very few memories of the campus. Dan and I visited the campus last month and it was almost all new to me. I didn't recognize the library, the very large chapel, the archways, or any of the other large landmarks. The only memories I had were of specific details. I remembered the purple flowers blooming on the gray brick of the chemistry building and the layout of the lab room where I worked.

I initially thought that I could predict which of my three groups my friends and family members fell into by knowing a bit about their powers of observation or their visual imagery. But I was wrong. My friend S is an expert on fossils, phylogeny, and Charles Darwin. He is a superb naturalist but his keen powers of observation do not extend to his sense of direction. He was completely stumped when I asked him where north was and happily confesses to being in the CLUELESS group.

. . .

Then there's my friend M, who is a bit scatterbrained. I thought she would be in the CLUELESS group too. . . . But, despite her absent-minded-professor persona, she always knows where north is.

Recently, while traveling by plane, I sat next to a commercial airline pilot of thirty years. I thought for sure he would be a NATURAL or, at the very least, a very competent BOY SCOUT, but when I asked him about his sense of direction, he laughed and said, "Talk to my kids about this! I have gotten them lost umpteen times. I can't find my way anywhere on the ground. In the air, it's different. I can see everything." The pilot actually fell into the CLUELESS category when walking or driving.

So has the hat helped to orient me? Yes, it has. But to get a better sense of direction, I have to think hard about what the hat is telling me. In the past . . . I tried to determine where I'd been by remembering how I moved my body while going from place to place. Most people rely more on their vision; at least other members of my family do.

I have always been surprised by the way Dan and the children turn on the room light before entering a room. If there is dim, ambient light illuminating the basic contours of a familiar setting, then I don't bother with extra light. I have unconsciously memorized how my body feels when moving through the rooms in our house. This dependence on a kinesthetic sense works fine in very familiar and confined locations, but it is not a good strategy for navigation in the wider world.

. . .

Some people have commented that using a GPS system or carrying a compass might work as well as my hat in developing my direction sense. I don't think I would have learned that much from a GPS system because it does all the work for me. Using a compass would be helpful, but, as you mentioned in your letter, the signal that I get from the hat, the buzzing I feel every time I turn my head north, gives me an immediate indication of the way I am moving. Finally, the fact that I move my head to get the buzzing puts me in an active role: If I want to "feel" north, I turn my head. The other day, I was walking north toward the library without my hat, and I realized I was expecting to feel the buzzing.

. . .

My mother was not cross-eyed, but we shared a similar visual style. She paid attention to the near field and to details and had a poor spatial sense. She probably would have fallen into the CLUELESS group. She told me once that she would get confused while driving down highways; she would lose track of which lane the car was in and feel like she might be driving off the road. I have had similar experiences.

In my mother's last years, she was always busy about the house. My brother, sister, and I would watch her move about with her Parkinson's shuffle and teetering balance and beg her to just sit down. But she never did, continuing her seemingly aimless puttering instead.

A year after my mother died, my father decided to move out of our house of forty-seven years. We found it surprisingly easy to empty the house of its contents. Everything was in its place. There was a little drawer filled just with shoelaces, another just with paper clips. Even the items in the basement were sorted and arranged in a logical manner.

I sometimes theorize that my mother's poor spatial sense compelled her to organize the house so thoroughly. Did her visual style drive her to all that puttering? Then I remember her thoughtfulness and wonder instead if her exquisite ordering of the house was the final gift she decided to leave her family.

. . .

Yours in a new direction,

Sue

I offered to make Oliver a compass hat but received the following response.

OLIVER SACKS, M.D.   5/31/09

2 HORATIO ST. #3G · NEW YORK, NY · 10014
TEL: 212.633.8373 · FAX: 212.633.8928
MAIL@OLIVERSACKS.COM

Dear Sue,

Thank you for your latest (and as always enthralling) letter.

I am fascinated by your "HAT" experiment and explorations, and (when I got your email offering such a HAT for me) first enthused "Yes, please!" But when I read your long letter I realized that exploring this new sense would be a major enterprise, as it is now for you—and I feel too beleaguered and pressed at the moment (by writing)* to be able to do anything else. If (as I hope) a completed draft gets off to the publisher by summer's end, I will feel in a much freer state of mind, and ready to try the HAT then.

. . .

See you soon?

[signature]

═══════

Oliver was right. I did spend hours, mostly while walking to and from work, thinking about our directional sense. In a letter written eight months later, on February 13, 2010, I described a simple, hat-less strategy for orientation. I had basically rediscovered for myself the sundial.

I drew a picture to show you my method for judging NORTH on a sunny day. Imagine that you are the person in the picture who is casting the shadow. If you are in the northern hemisphere, then north would be to the *right* of your shadow if it is morning and to the *left* of your shadow if it is afternoon. When the sun is close to overhead, your shadow points north. It's that simple, yet it took me hours of walking around with my compass hat to figure this out!

* Oliver was writing *The Mind's Eye* at the time.

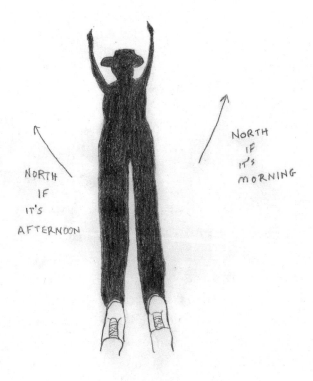

NORTH IF IT'S AFTERNOON

NORTH IF IT'S MORNING

I remain,

Yours with every step,

Sue

I never did give Oliver a compass hat, but he remained intrigued and amused by it, so much so that in June 2010, we made a video of me and the hat called "North!" and posted it on YouTube.*

---

* See youtube.com/watch?v=til_xXzq538. The videographer for "North!" was Dempsey Rice.

One Damn Thing After Another

In September 2009, Oliver phoned to encourage me to come to a retrospective show of his friend Gerald (Jerry) Marx's 3D Art. Jerry gave me and Rosalie a personal tour of his spectacular, depth-filled work, and then I headed to Greenwich Village to visit Oliver. He was writing about vision and hallucinations and was curious about my mother's hallucinations that were brought on by the long-term use of the drugs she took for Parkinson's disease. Partly because of Oliver's hearing loss and partly because we both think best through the act of writing, I answered his question in a letter. I told him that my mom, diagnosed with Parkinson's disease in 1985, saw Dr. S. in New York, who started her on Sinemet* in 1987.

> I can't remember how long after 1987 it was that my mother described to me her hallucinations, but I think it was at least five years. We were standing at the kitchen sink doing the dishes and looking out at the backyard when my mother pointed to the large oak tree and told me that there were four men sitting in the tree. When I told her that it wasn't so, she readily agreed

---

* Sinemet is used to treat Parkinson's disease and is a combination of levodopa and carbidopa. Levodopa is converted in the brain to dopamine, the neurotransmitter that is lacking in Parkinson's disease, whereas carbidopa prevents the levodopa from being broken down.

but said that she saw them there anyway. A few days later, as we went down to the carport to get into the car, she told me that there were three men in the backseat. Again, she knew that this was not the case, but she saw them as clear as day.[*]

When my mother described her hallucinated men, I had a mental image of identical, tall, thin, cartoon-like men in top hats. I never really thought about this particular image until talking with you last week. Then I realized the image came from an illustration by Jules Feiffer in Norton Juster's children's book *The Phantom Tollbooth*.[†] . . .

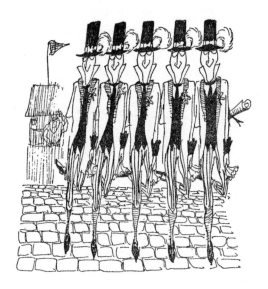

My mother did not seem particularly disturbed by her hallucinations, and I'm not sure she ever told Dr. S. about them. She may not even have mentioned them to my father, who worried and fussed over her constantly. Instead, she

---

[*] Oliver later told me that a common kind of hallucination involves one image, like the men my mother saw, repeated multiple times

[†] This illustration appears in chapter 3, "Welcome to Dictionopolis," when Milo enters Dictionopolis and is greeted by five identical tall men.

tolerated them with the same bemused attitude with which she approached all of her other medical problems. "Life," she used to say to me, "is just one damn thing after another."

Unfortunately, Oliver was about to enter a phase in his life that could be described as "one damn thing after another." Although, at my visit, he looked sturdy and strong (and very British) in his khaki shorts and hiking boots, he would soon go to the hospital for a complete knee replacement. So I sent him a lighthearted letter about crickets who hear with ears not on their head but on their knees. My letter crossed in the mail with a much more serious note from Oliver, dated September 29, 2009, and his was not good news.

OLIVER SACKS, M.D.
2 Horatio Street, 3G
New York, NY 10014
Tel: (212) 633-8373
Fax: (212) 633-8928

9/29/09

Dear Sue

wonderful

        Thank you for your (as always, wodefful) letter of a few
days ago - with its thoughts on STEREO and much else - and, of
course, the description of (some of) your mother's hallucinations
when on medication for parkinson's - hallucinations which she
recognkzed and described with humor and detachment (and which
you then empathically imaged as the imaginary creatures in
YHE PP_ANTOM TOO . TOLL BOO TH.

        Your letter (like almost you have writen me) wll be
invaluable when in helping me to arrive at an amneded and
enlarged version of S TEREO SUE (I won't make any substantial changes
- only additions), and my own story (which of course includes
' FLATLAND ', ' a world without space ' ' No room ' or whatveer
I should svbtitle this part..). I fear I have now lost what
little vision I had in the right eye - which, among other things,
gave me some ' implic t ' or uncoscious stereo in peripheral
vision - because I hayd a hemorrhage into the on Sunday, and
can see nothing but a sea of pink. I am told it will take 4-6
months to clear. So now I am truly monocular - and realize that
a futher essential sort of spatial sense and orientation has
disappeared - only now, in retrospect, do I realize how valuable
this was .. and what you call ' confabulations ' (I think you
mean ' conflations ') are more severe. I have difficulty recognizing
some buildings, because shadows cast by things in front of them and
behind them, and shafts of light and shadows, all get incoporated
into a complex (and unintelligible) flat abstract. The very
idea   of architecture, of objects, of empty space, or solidity,
seems even more eroded.. Interesting to write about, but unfortunate
it happened... [I have, however, an exciting idea about a ' new '
book (or, rather, a different rearrangement of writing } - so
that one book will be entirely   about HALLUCINATIONS, and the
oher will cosists of ? five individual case-histories - ' Anna O ',
                                        → frev

Pat, Two alexic witers (engel and Scribner),
STEREO SUE - and then - -- then me-

So your s tory, and my s tory, will be in direct _juxta_ apposition.

‹----------

    I am   taking the drafts of all these to hospital
(where I will probably be moreorless uncomscious, or stoned
on analgesics, for a couple of days) -and then (af we can
~~swing it with insurance~~) to a Rehab place - hopefully Burke -
where I may have a fair chance of quiet writing and revising,
with Kate's help. Ourthought is that the caes-history book
(TITLE UNCLEAR AS YET) can be got ito publishable shape
fairly quickly - even perhaps a month or so - and get published
(\f one is VEY lucky) next Spring... and I ca then take ~~more~~ MY
time over ~~(what would be~~ the larger and more complex HALLUCINATION
book.

                    OUT
    Anyhow these are _my_ thoughts at the monent...
                       ^

    Again, thank you, thank you for everything,

    and all m y love,

                                    Mon Oliver
                        ☺
                          (nor an evrhonion
                          on Steno Sue).

Oliver did not let this latest visual crisis stop his writing. Not in the least. He and Kate had decided that the vision stories he wanted to tell should be included in not one but two books, a shorter one with five case histories, including mine and his (*The Mind's Eye*), and a longer one about hallucinations (*Hallucinations*). His referral to his own story, "Flatland" in the letter became the chapter, "Persistence of Vision" in *The Mind's Eye*. The sign-off to this letter reads "MonoOliver (not as euphonious as Stereo Sue)."

Soon after being discharged from Burke Rehab, on October 18, 2009, Oliver wrote a nine-page, handwritten letter complete with his little drawings. He saw parallels between the therapy for his knee and the therapy for my vision, although his treatment was far more painful. As he wrote about this excruciating process and provided graphic descriptions of his swollen leg ("the leg looks like a pumpkin, or a bloated pig carcass"), his handwriting grew sloppier and sloppier, and the ink from his Montblanc fountain pen smeared all the more. Here's a copy of his letter, with a transcription of his handwriting.

OLIVER SACKS, M.D.
2 HORATIO ST. #3G · New York, NY · 10014
TEL: 212.633.8373 · FAX: 212.633.8928
MAIL@OLIVERSACKS.COM

(2)

(Back to my old MontBlanc fountain pen — but one is now taken for ever to dry ... and blotting-paper seems to be virtually obsolete).

Rehab has been 'steady' (if such a term can be applied to a stepwise process ⌐_ , not a gradual one ___ ~) etc — Of course. these are qualitative steps — not just an extra 3° of flexion, but a whole different organization (like moving from a walker to a cane), and cannot even be conceived from the step one is on. I suppose this is analogous to learning, education, Vygotsky's "Zone of Proximal Development" (ZPD)

(Back to my old Montblanc fountain pen—but the ink takes forever to dry—and blotting paper seems to be virtually obsolete).

Rehab has been "steady" (if such a term can be applied to a stepwise process, and not a graded one etc. Of course, there are <u>qualitative</u> steps—not just an extra 3° of flexion, but a whole different organization (like moving from a walker to a cane), and cannot even be conceived from the step one is on.

I suppose this is analogous to learning, education, Vygotsky's "zone of proximal development."*

I understood exactly what Oliver meant when he wrote that each therapy step, such as moving with a walker to moving with a cane, required a whole new organization. I had experienced the same transformations with vision therapy. So, on October 26, 2009, I wrote back,

With vision therapy, I was able to learn new eye movements, but only because these eye movements were incorporated into larger, purposeful acts. Many ophthalmologists have told me that my acquisition of stereopsis is impossible because "you can't teach an esotrope how to diverge."†

---

* Lev Vygotsky (1896–1934) was a Soviet psychologist who developed the concept of the zone of proximal development. This refers to a developmental stage in children when they are not capable of learning a skill on their own but can learn it with help from an adult or knowledgeable peer. The skill is just beyond their abilities.

† An esotrope is a person with crossed eyes, whereas "diverge," in this context, means to straighten the eyes after they are turned in.

No one taught me how to diverge. Instead I learned how to fuse and then to maintain fusion while looking at objects farther and farther away.

Oliver's October 18 letter continued by describing his relationship with his therapists:

The Rehab people at Burke were marvelous—the relationship (it seems to me) was as much one of TEACHER/STUDENT as THERAPIST/PATIENT. (I would like to write about this one day—it was a subject I scarcely touched, and perhaps represented as mostly "spontaneous" in A LEG TO STAND ON.) And, of course, <u>your</u> experience, and <u>your</u> book, is about LEARNING to see, whatever the Hubel/Wiesel <u>mechanisms</u>[*] involved.

His remarks reminded me of a friend's therapy story. My October 26 letter continued:

You write about the therapists at Burke being more like teachers than therapists. I think of a good therapist as a good coach. My friend has a daughter, K., with cerebral palsy. By the time K. turned ten, she had grown quite heavy and was having a hard time getting around on her crutches. She had been going to physical therapy, but the therapy was not very effective. Her parents then hired for her a physical therapist who was also a personal trainer and this changed everything. In K.'s mind, people with injuries and

---

[*] David Hubel (1926–2013) and Torsten Wiesel (born 1924) were pioneers in the study of the visual cortex and worked out the response properties of many of the visual cortical cells to light. They demonstrated that some cells were monocular, but most were binocular.

disabilities see physical therapists, but the rich and famous have personal trainers who come to their home. K. worked hard with her trainer, stuck to her diet, slimmed down, and worked up to walking one mile per day.

Knee replacement, as Oliver described in his October 18 letter, presented sensory as well as mechanical problems.

> Once I got on my feet I found, as do all patients with total joint replacement, <u>sensory</u> as well as mechanical problems. One no longer has any joint receptors (for proprioception or pain), because one no longer has a living joint. And proprioception in surrounding tissues is compromised because of the gross edema—so the leg is naturally heavy, but different in sensation (in my case there were some residual sensory deficits from muscle-nerve damage in '74). But one accommodates to this—maybe recruit other receptors, or just put what sensory information one has to better use.

As Dan, my robot-building husband, knows, even a robot can't move well without feedback to tell it how it is moving. So, when I wrote to Oliver on November 21, 2009, about proprioception, I discussed its role in my vision therapy, as well as wondering if there was a way he could enhance his proprioceptive feedback for walking.

> When I went through optometric vision therapy, I was made aware of the way that I saw and learned what it *felt like* to move my eyes in new and different ways. Unlike some strabismics, I never knew with which eye I was fixating. Using red/green glasses and red/green targets, I discovered that I continually switched fixation and learned how it felt to "turn on" both eyes at the same time. The greatest epiphany

for me, however, was the way it felt to converge and diverge my eyes in order to bi-fixate beads at different distances along the Brock string. Over and over again, I memorized how my eyes felt when I mastered a new task.

My tennis teacher also used a kinesthetic approach when teaching me how to serve a tennis ball. After I learned how to toss the ball upward and hit it, he had me repeat the movements with my eyes closed so that I had to pay attention to the proprioceptive feel of the movements.

All these vision/tennis training experiences bring me back to a sweet memory of my daughter Jenny when she was an infant. I had dressed her in bright red socks, laid her down on her back on our big bed next to Dan, and was about to leave when Dan called me back excitedly. Jenny had just discovered her feet! While waving her feet in the air, she had caught them in her field of view. She looked completely startled, then got the feet back into view, and wiggled them. She did this again and again, laughing with pure delight. She had connected the *feeling* of moving her feet with the *act* of moving her feet, just as I, seventeen years later, was to connect the feeling of making vergence movements of my eyes with the act of bi-fixating a bead on a string.

I wonder if a sort of proprioceptive training could work for you today. Your somatosensory cortex* must be in a state of flux, since the input from your knee joint is no longer present. Perhaps, with selective muscle vibration, you could expand somatosensory and motor cortical representation of the proprioceptors in the muscles right around the knee joint, and this expansion might improve coordination. Maybe, you could get a whole new feel for walking.

---

* The somatosensory cortex is a region of the brain that processes sensory information from across the body, including proprioception, touch, temperature, and pain.

Oliver's difficulties with his legs and eyes led to a whole, new perspective on his Greenwich Village neighborhood as he described further in his long October 18 letter. He also saw analogies between his loss of awareness of 3D space and the space to his far right, both consequences of losing vision in his right eye.

I can now (18 days after surgery) walk moderately steadily, albeit cautiously, with a cane—but only <u>indoors</u>, if I am allowed. I need someone with me if I go out into bustling Horatio St. with the crunch of inattentive (functionally deafferented) people totally engrossed in text-messaging, speaking on cell phones etc; people suddenly bursting out of shops and doorways—people with dogs on long leashes—often tiny insect-like dogs, which repel each other mutually, like electrified particles, so that their leash, like trip-wires, stick out at 180°.

And all this is MUCH (<u>MUCH!</u>) worse now I am completely blind in the right eye, and have lost a big chunk (~50–60°) of my visual field to that side. Only now do I realize how crucial that crescent of peripheral vision was, not only for a sort of "inferior" stereoscopy, but for the perception, the <u>idea</u>, of an extended (a 2D extended) visual space.

I am continually taken aback by people (and objects) "coming out of the blue" on my right side. If I am with Kate, say, get into an elevator, and am puzzled because I cannot see her—I think she is talking with the doorman, made a detour to the mailbox, something—remain puzzled until she says something, and then realize that she is on my right, beyond my visual horizon, and that she must have entered the elevator <u>with</u> me, to my right—in the missing or "blind" segment of my visual field: but what startles her is not only my failure to <u>see</u> her—that is straightforward—but my failure to conceive (or imagine) it—so the peripheral field loss is suspiciously like a <u>central</u> one (a partial hemianopia)—"out of sight, out of mind" is usually applied to something like candies which will be eaten unless they are hidden—but it applies equally (even spectacularly) here—the loss of visual field (the field) goes with a loss of "mental" field, of "the mind's eye." One can realize that <u>intellectually</u> (as you were forced, when in college, to confront your own loss/lack of stereoscopy) and accommodate (turning one's head or eye to the blind segment—using monocular cues). Indeed one must (or one is in big trouble)—but it is only intellectual or (better) behavioural—the loss of (the sense of) 3D space with loss of stereo seems to me analogous to this loss of a segment of "rightness"—a sort of hemi-inattention or hemi-agnosia or neglect—with the (sudden) loss of vision in one eye.

Forgive this outrageously long letter—the pain makes me verbose—but also you are my favorite correspondent now.

love Oly

Creatures of the Couch

Among all the creatures in the world, Oliver's favorites were cephalopods—nautilus, squid, octopus, and cuttlefish. Their bodies, with their many arms and tentacles, may be very different from our own, but with their large eyes and big brains, they are like us, too. A few years back, I had given Oliver a stuffed cephalopod toy, a handsome orange squid that I often saw perched (if a squid can perch) on the back of his living room sofa. So, while he was in rehab in October 2009, I sent him another stuffed cephalopod, this time, a blue octopus.

> I thought that there may be times when you, with a new, hard knee joint, wished you were an octopus instead. The only hard part of these creatures is the beak located in the mouth. They are so flexible that they can bend themselves into crannies and crevices, and, best of all, they get to swim all day.

Yes, Oliver wrote back, the squid had been lonely and was very glad to have a companion. "Maybe sometime a woolly *Sepia** will join them."

---

* *Sepia* is the scientific name for a genus of cuttlefish. The reddish-brown color sepia is named for the brown pigment from the ink sac of these cuttlefish.

Nerves of Steel

Yet, Oliver's troubles had not yet peaked. His next letter, written on December 1, 2009, was in a very slanted, shaky hand.

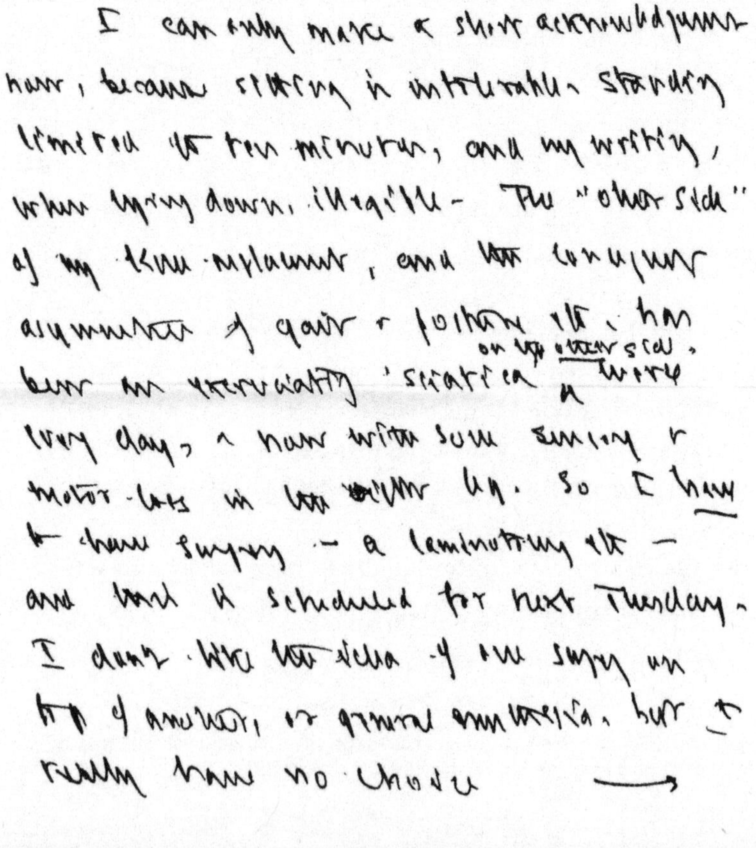

I can only make a short acknowledgement now, because sitting is intolerable, standing limited to ten minutes, and my writing, when lying down, illegible. The "other side" of my knee replacement, and the consequent asymmetries of gait & posture etc., has been an excruciating 'sciatica' on the other side, worse every day, & now with some sensory & motor loss in the other leg. So I have to have surgery — a laminectomy etc — and have it scheduled for next Thursday. I don't like the idea of one surgery on top of another, or general anaesthesia, but I really have no choice →

I can only make a short acknowledgment now, because sitting is intolerable, standing limited to ten minutes, and my writing, when lying down, illegible. The "other side" of my knee-replacement, and the consequent asymmetry of gait and posture etc., has been an irritating sciatica on the <u>other</u> side, worse every day, and now with some sensory and motor loss in the other leg. So I <u>have</u> to have surgery—a laminectomy etc—and had it scheduled for next Thursday. I don't like the idea of one surgery on top of another, or general anesthesia, but I really have no choice.

Oliver and his cascade of misfortunes reminded me of the biblical Job, but despite it all, and with the help of Kate and his office assistant Hailey Wojcik, he continued to write letters and had finished a draft of *The Mind's Eye*. Soon, he wrote, he would send me the manuscript.

I had been feeling at a loss for letters to write that might cheer Oliver up. But his struggles with incapacitating sciatica reminded me of a hopeful story that I knew intimately.

December 11, 2009

Dear Oliver,

I hope your surgery has brought you some relief and gradually you'll be able to return to a more active life. Your last letter with descriptions of your debilitating sciatica reminded me of another story, one that took place ten years ago and had a happy ending.

My mother was severely osteoporotic. She broke many bones in her wrist and shoulder and broke her ribs fourteen times, but the worst breaks were the compression fractures of her spine. Two such fractures left her completely immobile. She was not paralyzed, but all movement brought her great pain. She could lie comfortably only on her back. If she moved at all, her leg would spasm, the muscles contracting into a steel-like mass that was excruciatingly painful. For five months, she lay unmoving in bed. I had to diaper her. It was a very difficult time.

My father and I took my mother to many doctors, both in their local Connecticut town and in New York City, but no one knew what to do other than prescribe OxyContin. A trip to the doctor was a major expedition, since we had to take my mother on a stretcher in an ambulance. The thirteenth doctor we saw specialized in managing pain. Ironically, her office was on the second floor of an office building, and the elevator was too small to accommodate a full-length stretcher. We had to bend my mother into a sitting position, setting off her spasms. All of this, she bore with great stoicism.

At our visit, the pain doctor seemed distracted and aloof but, fortunately, had a habit of thinking out loud. I heard her murmur, "pressure points, epidural, botulinum toxin." She did a small manipulation that had no effect and told us to return in a few weeks. But to someone like my mother, suffering from unrelenting pain, a few weeks is an eternity. We left the doctor's office feeling frustrated, disappointed, and depressed.

After settling my mother back at her home, I boarded the train for the return trip to Massachusetts and thought back to the doctor's visit. I kept thinking about botulinum toxin. If Botox[*] blocks neuromuscular transmission, could an injection in the right spot inhibit the muscle spasms and allow the nerves to heal? So I called the pain doctor's office and spoke to the very competent receptionist who told me that the pain doctor was not yet licensed for Botox use but another local doctor, a physiatrist named Dr. F., was. When I

---

[*] Botox is another name for botulinum toxin.

called Dr. F.'s office, I got a message machine, so I left a message, then put my cell phone away, and closed my eyes to nap for the rest of the train ride.

A few minutes later, I was kicking myself. During that period, when I left messages for doctors about my mother, I would say something like, "This is Dr. Sue Barry calling about a patient Estelle Feinstein." There was nothing inaccurate about this message, but it was meant to deceive. Since I have a PhD, I can call myself "doctor" though I rarely do, but I had found that physicians were more likely to return my calls promptly if they thought I was an MD. When speaking to Dr. F.'s answering machine, I had simply given my name and indicated that I was calling about my mother.

During the train trip home, it had snowed for the umpteenth time that winter, so upon reaching the house, I decided that shoveling the snow might be therapeutic. I had cleared about half the driveway when my daughter shouted from the house that I had a phone call. I told her to take a message, but Jenny informed me that the caller was on my cell phone. Cell phones were new, at least to me back then, and very few people had my number. I put down my snow shovel and went up to the house hoping it would be the doctor.

Indeed, it was good Dr. F. returning my call. I told her about my mother and asked her if she thought botulinum toxin might help. She told me that she had never used Botox in the way I proposed, but she would be willing to give it a try. When I began to describe how we would transport my mother to her office, Dr. F. cut me off, saying she would not ask my mother to come to her—she would come to my parents' house.

Two days later, Dr. F. visited my parents, armed with syringes filled with the life-giving toxin. She gave my mother

several injections at the site where the spasms began. After
one week, my father called to say that the spasms were less
frequent. Another week or two passed, and the spasms had
completely disappeared. Gradually, my mother was able to
sit up, stand, and walk. Since she had Parkinson's disease,
her walk was really just a shuffle around the house with her
walker. But that was enough. The spasms and pain never
returned.

There is an epilogue to this tale. When I lecture, I try to
include little vignettes to keep my students engaged. So, in
my neurobiology class, I teach the mechanics of
neurotransmitter release and the mechanism of Botox's
action, using the story about my mother and the poison. As I
talk, I can sense that every student is listening intently.
Sometime later, when I give an exam, I find that every single
student demonstrates a detailed understanding of
transmitter release and Botox's effects. Of course, I'm using a
strategy that I learned from reading your books. When it
comes to teaching, there's simply no substitute for a
compelling story.

Get well soon!

Love,

Sue

Whenever Oliver seemed in need of a "cheer up" gift, and I had
no more stuffed cephalopods to offer, I sent him something musical. I had already given him *Violin Dreams* and later *Note by Note*,
a wonderful book by Tricia Tunstall, about teaching piano. This
time, I sent him a stunning DVD of Glenn Gould playing Bach's
Goldberg Variations. In return, Oliver wrote, "I watched, listened,

and (like you) was overwhelmed by the DVD of Gould revisiting the Goldberg Variations. One can *see* his passions, his ecstasy (and his spontaneity and sense of humor—the charming hand-movements *between* variations etc—wonderful!"

On Christmas Eve day, 2009, Rosalie, Temple Grandin, and I visited Oliver at his apartment. He looked frighteningly thin, which had compelled a friend who owned a restaurant to send him calorie-rich food every night. Oliver told us that the pain from the sciatica had been so bad he had contemplated suicide. His pain, like my mother's, was caused by a crushed nerve and did not respond well to opiate drugs. Oliver even mentioned my mother's botulinum toxin story to his doctor, who assured him his pain would ebb with time. And now it was finally lifting. He could sit for ten-minute periods, dictated by a kitchen timer, but paced the apartment or lay down on his bed for the rest of the time. Nevertheless, we shared a meal and exchanged stories, reminding me of Oliver's considerable strength and endurance. And he had not stopped writing and revising. He sent me home with a draft of his autobiographical chapter for his upcoming book *The Mind's Eye*.

It was a memorable train trip home, not only because I had Oliver's memoir to read but also because the conductor sang in a rich bass voice "I'll Be Home for Christmas" as he passed through each car, collecting tickets. But, despite the conductor's jubilance, I grew increasingly sad as Oliver described his losses—he could no longer see or was even conscious of a large area to his right, and the only time he could see with stereopsis was in his dreams or when he smoked dope (which he always called by its scientific name cannabis). Dreams and drugs. This intrigued me because my first views with stereopsis had a hallucinatory feel and reminded me of a passage in a book I had recently read. So, in my next letter, dated December 28, 2009, I wrote,

When reading Huxley's *The Doors of Perception*, I was really
struck by the objects he chose to describe when he was high
on mescalin. He wrote about the exact same objects that first
startled me when I began to see in 3D. He talked of flowers
in a vase, a chair and its legs, and the folds in his trousers.
I, too, was really taken by the solidity of plants and flowers,
by the way chairs displayed themselves in space, and the
luxurious pleats and grooves in my family's winter coats.

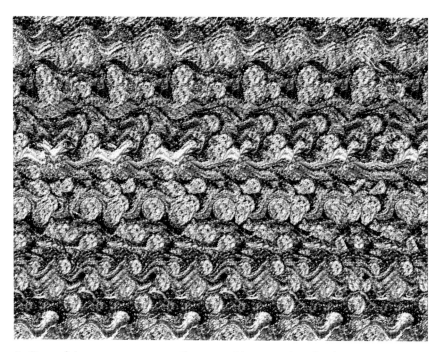

1. One of the autostereograms I sent to Oliver on October 10, 2005: To reveal the Magic Eye® 3D illusion, hold the center of this picture *right up to your nose*. It should be blurry. Focus as though you are looking *through* the picture into the distance. *Very slowly* move the picture away from your face until you begin to perceive depth. Now hold the picture still and the hidden illusion should slowly appear. The longer you look, the clearer the illusion becomes.

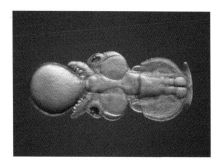

2. This embryo of the squid *Doryteuthis pealeii* is only 2.4 millimeters long.

3. Cycad anaglyph: To see the 3D, use red/green lenses with the green lens over the right eye.

4. Anaglyph of a random dot stereogram by Bela Julesz: While wearing red/green lenses and with the red lens over the right eye, you should see a central square floating forward. Put the green lens over the right eye, and the central square will recede behind the page.

5. My father's self-portrait

6. Me, Theresa Ruggiero, and Oliver, in Dr. Ruggiero's vision therapy room

7. From left to right: Theresa Ruggiero; Oliver; my son, Andy; me; and Bob Wasserman, at Spoleto restaurant. Not pictured: Ralph Siegel, who took the photograph.

8. Oliver and me in Oliver's apartment

9. The Compass Hat

"Stereo Sue" Revisited

A month later, on January 30, 2010, I wrote Oliver a long letter requesting that, for the chapter in *The Mind's Eye*, he change four sentences in the original "Stereo Sue." These changes referred back to a discussion we'd had when "Stereo Sue" was first written. Oliver had originally speculated that my ability to gain 3D vision was dependent upon a few brief stereoviews I might have experienced when young. As I had argued four years earlier, I wrote that these brief stereo experiences may not have been critical to my developing stereopsis in midlife. Almost all of us, including people with infantile strabismus, are probably born with circuitry for binocular vision and stereopsis. This circuitry, however, is suppressed if one is cross-eyed and cannot point the two eyes at the same spatial location. "I think these [childhood] stereoviews indicated that I had the potential for stereovision all along and that it required proper posturing of my eyes to bring it out."

Oliver answered my letter a few days later, on February 4, 2010.

I just read your (superb!) letter, and hasten to reply (tho' I do not even have any proper stationery).

This letter was written on a yellow legal pad.

> I take all your points, am more than grateful for the careful thinking which all of them show. . . . So (barring one tiny thing) I am happy to accept all your suggestions.

What was that "one tiny thing?" Words were important and powerful to Oliver:

> (The tiny thing is the word "posture," which you use several times, and suggest I use.) I will have to find an alternative. For to me (this may reflect the fact that I am elderly English) the verb "posture" has an overwhelming meaning of behaving falsely, putting on a false front—it is very close to "imposture." Your use may be technically correct, but I could not bring myself to use the word in this connection.

So, Oliver used the word "position" instead.

Barium Birthday

A day before my birthday, which is February 20, Oliver sent a letter written on a yellow legal pad.

Oliver Sacks, M.D.
2 Horatio Street #3G
New York, NY 10014

Dear Sue,

Almost everyone I know is having
a birthday around now, and I
have tried to send people their
birthday elements (so I got an
Ingot of indium for Billy's 49th, and
a pebble of thulium for my sister-in-law's
(69th). I wish I could send you
some caesium for your 55th — it
is, at room temperature, a pale golden
liquid — like golden mercury — but it
is also the most dangerous element to have
around if it gets loose — it catches
fire instantly, burning with a caerulean
flame and ~~if you heat~~ it

twenty water causes a violent explosion,

and (the oxygen of) sand only

fuels its fury. And ~~cesium~~ ~~is~~ keep

an't find any pure

cesium minerals —

So no cesium ~~this~~ this year —

but barytes next year.

Happy Birthday!

love.

ous

You would need

a fire-extinguisher

full of argon

PS   new

I discover, in fact,

that you were born in '5~~5~~

summer in

(I think the ~~autumn~~ of 1955 — 55

~~so~~ seduced me).

February 19, 2010

Dear Sue,

Almost everyone I know is having a birthday around now,
and I have tried to send people their birthday elements (so
I got an ingot of indium for Billy's 49th, and a pebble of
thulium for my sister-in-law's 69th). I wish I could send you
some caesium for your 55th—it is, at room temperature, a
pale golden liquid—like golden mercury—but, it is also the
most dangerous element to have around if it gets loose—
it catches fire instantly, burning with a cerulean flame.
Throwing water causes a violent explosion, and (the oxygen
of) sand only feeds its fury. And there are few, if any, pure
caesium minerals.

So no caesium this year, but baryta next year.

Happy Birthday,

You would need
a fire-extinguisher
full of argon.

Yours—

Oliver

PS—I discover, in fact, that you were born in '54 (I think the
symmetry of 1955–55 seduced me).

Oliver then had a mineralogist friend send me three lovely, trans-
lucent blue, prismatic barite (barium sulfate) crystals. They now hold
a special place in my rock and mineral collection.

Ideal Reader

Dear Oliver,

During the first week of April, I went camping and whale watching in Baja, Mexico, gave some talks in Los Angeles— and also read *The Calculus of Friendship*.*

I liked the book on many levels. First, of course, was the description of a friendship that developed, like ours, through letters. Then, there was the math—some of which I worked out with pencil and paper. Reading about the Fibonacci and Fourier series was like rediscovering old friends. In fact, the very first conversation I had with Dan was on Fourier transforms. I didn't know anything about Fourier analysis at the time (this was 1976), and he explained it all to me. He was so earnest, enthusiastic, and gentle that I fell deeply in love with him right then and there and saved the little scrap of paper that he had covered with waveforms and mathematical symbols.

---

* The author of *The Calculus of Friendship* is Steven Strogatz.

Now, thirty-four years later, I was in the LA airport reading about the Fourier series in Strogatz's book. My mathematical daughter was sitting beside me, so I showed her the chapter and mentioned that I once had been enamored of another series, the Taylor series, but now could not remember the details. Just as in Strogatz's book, student and teacher changed places. Jenny showed me how to work out the Taylor expansion for the sine and cosine functions and thus allowed me to rediscover their connection to e^{ix} and Euler's identity.

All through the trip, Strogatz's ideas filtered into my experiences. I loved his broad definition of empathy (page 13). While whale watching, we not only felt strong empathy for the whales but had the distinct impression that they had empathy for us. Our empathic feelings were heightened by the fact that most of the whales we saw were mother/calf pairs who swam in parallel, so close to each other that they almost touched. Once we saw a tired baby whale resting across his mother's broad back. Who wouldn't want such an enormous, protective mother?

Gray whales weigh 700 pounds at birth. During the first two weeks of life, they gain three pounds <u>per hour</u> feasting on their mother's milk, an elixir far richer than ice cream for it is 50 percent milk fat. Newborn whales may be enormous, but a baby is still a baby. So, when one of these giant infants swam toward our boat, we all lapsed into high-pitched baby talk crying, "Here whale! Here little one!" The whales seemed to like our calls, and one mother pushed her baby up toward the boat to be petted. The baby's skin felt just like the wet surface of a shelled, hard-boiled egg.

You and the gray whales would feel great empathy for each other. With their eyes positioned far to the sides of their

heads, they probably do not have binocular vision. They
made large head turns to look directly at us. After breaching,
they usually come down on their right side and over time
lose vision in their right eye. In *Moby Dick*, my brother
pointed out to me, Melville wrote about the timidity of
sperm whales, a trait that he ascribed to the position of their
eyes and their way of seeing.

. . .

I hope you are feeling better and writing with
enthusiasm. Since you are more or less housebound, I've
enclosed a shell (a bent-nosed Macoma—I think) that I
collected during my stay on the Baja peninsula. As you can
see, the shells there are very thick and sturdy—and some
contain little surprises inside.[*]

Yours to the letter,

Sue

OLIVER SACKS, M.D.
2 HORATIO ST. #3G · NEW YORK, NY · 10014
TEL: 212.633.8373 · FAX: 212.633.8928
MAIL@OLIVERSACKS.COM

May 4, 2010

Dear Sue,

Thank you for your (as always) wonderful letter (of 4/19)—
you are an amazing letter-writer—and each of your letters
brings something new and fresh.

---

[*] The surprises were smooth Mexican beach pebbles.

Indeed I think you should write <u>to</u> Strogatz—he is a very warm, friendly man, as well as greatly gifted—give him your personal resonances to his book. You are his ideal reader.

. . .

Thank you for the lovely shell, and its surprise inside— do write to Strogatz.

Thanks to Oliver, I did write to Steven Strogatz and visited him at his office at Cornell when I gave a lecture there. We chatted about two of his books, *The Calculus of Friendship* and *Sync*, and how we had each met Oliver.

Learning to Hear

J ust as Oliver learned from his patients, I learned from my students and wrote to Oliver about them, especially those who had overcome sensory deficits.

Oct. 11, 2014

Dear Oliver,

. . .

A few weeks ago, one of my students named P. bounded into my office with her ponytail bouncing behind her. "You look happy. You're wearing your hair differently," I said to her. P. is partially deaf and used to cover her ears with her hair to hide her hearing aids, but, on this day, her hair was pulled back, and I couldn't see any hearing aids at all. When I asked her what happened to them, P. quickly reached up and removed a tiny object from inside one ear and then showed me how the parts of the aid that hung around her outer ear were transparent. When she put the hearing aid back in her ear, the external parts seemed to disappear. But the hearing aids had improved her life in more ways than just appearance. "I love technology," P. said. "My hearing aids keep improving. For the first time, I can tell where a sound comes from. I don't have to do this"—and then she opened her eyes wide and moved her head back and forth as if to scan the scene in what was obviously a very practiced move. "When I hear a sound, I don't have to look for it. I just know where the sound is coming from." I thought this was spectacular—that P. could develop a new skill, sound localization, shortly after acquiring better auditory input— auditory input that presumably allowed her to distinguish at which ear the sound first arrived.

One of my most inspiring students, Zohra Damji, did not hear at all until she received a cochlear implant at age twelve, an age considered quite old for learning to hear for the first time. One day, when Zohra came to my office to drop off an assignment, I asked her, somewhat hesitantly, if she would tell me her story. She was very anxious to do so. We had many conversations together, and on April 19, 2010, I wrote to Oliver about them.

Two days ago, I had a long conversation with my student Zohra, the student who has been profoundly deaf since birth but received a cochlear implant at age 12. When her implant was first turned on, she did not recognize a sound as a sound but rather as a terrifying, unpleasant, unnerving feeling. For the first few days, she had this same frightening sensation every time she put on the implant. Eventually, she said, she came to accept the feeling. Then she began to expect the sensations and to interpret some of them as meaningful sounds.

I was intrigued by her use of the word "accept," because I think anyone who goes through a substantial perceptual improvement must learn to tolerate a certain amount of discomfort, uncertainty, and confusion. If one doesn't have the support of doctors, therapists, family, and/or friends, then one may not *allow* the changes to occur. One optometrist recently told me of her patient, a young man with amblyopia, who undertook vision therapy but was afraid that he'd develop stereovision during school. While studying for his exams, he wouldn't let himself see in this new way. Shortly after he left school for home and vacation, the world popped out for him in 3D.

Zohra told me that the first sounds she recognized were those of car motors and human speech, although it took her one to two months before she could distinguish male from female voices. You'll like this—the first word she could recognize by sound was—BANANA! Initially, she discriminated words by the number of syllables and by their distinctiveness. There are not many other English words that sound like banana!

I asked her what sounds surprised her, and she mentioned that she didn't expect that soft or compliant things, including paper, skin, and water, would make sounds. She was very surprised by the following:

- the sound of crinkling paper

- the sound of cutting paper with scissors

- the swishing sound of her clothes when she moves (initially very disturbing to her)

- the sound of her own, small body as she shifts her weight on a chair

- the sound of brushing her teeth

- the sound of a broom sweeping the floor

- the sound of water boiling

- the squeaking sound when she rubs her hand on a mirror

- the sound of chalk on a blackboard

- the sound of putting a key in a lock

- the sound of a pencil or pen when she writes on paper

- the helpful fact that you can learn that you've dropped something because it makes a sound when it hits the floor

- the sound of scratching her own skin

- the sound of a bowling ball rolling toward the pins in a bowling alley

- the sound of water coming out of a faucet

Zohra often had to ask what these new sounds were and is still delighted by new auditory discoveries. Since she can't wear her implant while bathing, I asked her if she had heard the sound of water going down a drain. She said she had not, so, twice, we filled up my office sink with water and listened as the water drained out. Zohra was intrigued and I was thrilled—I had introduced her to a new sound!

Zohra is captivated by echoes that make her voice sound different when she is in a large room versus a small, tiled bathroom. She recently noticed that her mother's voice on the phone sounds different when her mother has a cold and that people's voices sound odd when they first awaken. She was very surprised to learn that it's harder to hear a voice if the person is far away. Perhaps there's not a good analogy here with vision. If one has normal or corrected-to-normal acuity, distant objects don't look blurry; they just look smaller. In contrast, distant sounds appear muffled.

The biggest surprise however was learning that she can hear the emotion in a person's voice. She can hear anger, sadness, and laughter, and, most important, these sensations evoke a strong response in her. When she hears someone crying, she instantly feels sympathy but doesn't usually want to cry herself. But when she hears laughter, she wants to laugh, too. She never had this feeling when she saw but could not hear a person laughing. She had no idea that sounds could have such large effects on her mood or that so much meaning, information, and emotion is conveyed through the rhythms and dynamics of speech.

As Zohra was speaking about this, there were some students chatting away in the hall just outside my office. Zohra could not understand their words but loved the sounds, the ebb and flow of emotions conveyed by their voices. It made her feel more connected and more loved. Babies, she reminded me, are comforted by soothing words even though they don't understand them. People's voices are usually soothing to her. She must have felt terribly isolated when she could not hear.

Now that she can understand speech and speak well herself, I asked Zohra if she thinks by talking to herself. She does not. She does not look at a written word and then hear it in her head. While she can imagine environmental sounds like car motors, word sounds are more ephemeral. One exception is the word "stop." Once, after receiving her implant, she narrowly avoided being hit by a car when her mother yelled "Stop!" Zohra can now hear the word "Stop" in her head.

Zohra could not explain to me how she thinks. When she thinks about one of my lectures, for example, she recalls the meaning of the lesson but not my individual words. In

Seeing Voices, you describe "inner speech" and quote
Vygotsky as describing it as speech without words, as
thinking in pure meaning. This is what Zohra describes. I am
also reminded of my friend's daughter, K., who lost her sight
in her teens from retinitis pigmentosa. K. loves reading
Braille and teaching me some of the letters. I asked her what
she thinks when she feels, for example, the Braille letter A.
Does she see the shape of an A in her head or imagine the
way it feels? K. could not explain her perception.

To all this Oliver responded,

I was entranced with your detailed listing of the sounds
which astonished your student with a cochlear implant—
your depiction, her experience, of the whole course from
frightening and unintelligible and unprecedented sensation
to a world of meaningful (and sometimes beautiful)
sound(s)—and I <u>strongly</u> think (the two of) you should
"write it up"—as a piece, if not a short book—it is amazing
material—and there is not that much (worth reading) on the
origin of perceptions (in adults), their honing from noise to
signal.

With Oliver's encouragement, I did write up Zohra's story, incorporating it into my second book, which also included an account
of a young man named Liam who gained sight at age fifteen. Just as
Oliver often spent years communicating and visiting with his subjects, I spent an additional eleven years getting to know Zohra, Liam,
and their families before publishing *Coming to Our Senses: A Boy Who
Learned to See, A Girl Who Learned to Hear, and How We All Discover
the World.*

Iridium Birthday

July 9, 2010

Here is a pet cuttlefish to add to the cephalopodic menagerie
on your living room sofa. I thought about including a letter
about your wonderful new book, but the cuttlefish insisted
that the missive be only about your birthday and himself. He is
a very cunning cuttlefish who changes his colors and patterns
only when he thinks you are not looking. You will have to be
very clever (or perhaps smoking cannabis) to see this.

HAPPY, HAPPY BIRTHDAY, Oliver!

Yes, indeed, Oliver agreed in his thank-you note, the stuffed toy
cuttlefish changed its color, skin patterns, and textures, but only
when he wasn't looking.

Thoughts While Reading
The Mind's Eye

About this time, on June 21, 2010, Kate sent me a draft of *The Mind's Eye* to proofread. The book, of course, was written in complete sentences, not, as in Oliver's letters, with different thoughts bracketed by dashes and dots. In proofreading however, I often found commas inserted where they were not required. When I pointed these out, Kate told me that Oliver insisted on those commas to remind the reader to pause; the commas framed a thought.

While reading, I was particularly struck by the last chapter, which described visual imagery in people who are blind, imagery that ranged from almost nonexistent to vivid and lifelike. The same range is found in sighted people, and this led to a letter exchange with Oliver during the summer of 2010 about our personal visual imagery—or lack thereof. When I imagine the periodic table, for example, I see in my mind's eye the columns and rows as displayed in a standard chemistry textbook, and with concentration, I can mentally fill in the abbreviations in the boxes for the first thirty elements. If I am calculating in my head, I see numbers on a mental blackboard. But Oliver did not have pictures in his head: "Apropos of the Periodic Table," he wrote to me, "I think I have <u>logical</u> pictures of the

Group, the Periods, and the Periodicities (2, 8, 8, 18, 32 etc) which go with filling the electron shells. . . . With mental calculations I used to be extremely quick, but there was no 'mental blackboard' and not much 'inner speech.'" Did we solve these problems then in different ways or were there underlying mechanisms that we shared but that emerged differently when brought to consciousness?

The second chapter in *The Mind's Eye*, "Recalled to Life," made me think about the importance of loved ones for recovery and rehabilitation. Pat, one of Oliver's patients who had aphasia, developed a way to communicate without speech, but this couldn't have happened if Pat's devoted daughters had not been there to encourage her and to "listen." I read this chapter one morning and thought about it throughout the day, particularly about the daughters who were so caring and loving. I was taking care of my father at the time and did not always feel that I was as diligent and devoted as I could be. So that evening, July 19, 2010, I sat down and wrote an essay about caring for my dad.

Dad

On the morning of July 14, 2006, two days after his 84th birthday, my father woke up feeling deeply depressed. A few years earlier, he had moved to a retirement village close to my house, and, until that morning, he seemed content and engaged. The raw grief following my mother's death had passed; he had made new friends and drove his car regularly to the lumber and art supply stores where he bought materials to build his large canvases and paint.

That my father should have strong feelings and reactions was not surprising. He is an artist who has always lived intensely, being quick to anger, wildly creative, and passionate about his violin. He was a far more exciting dad, I felt, than the more reserved and conservative fathers of some of my friends. But now, my father seemed to have lost all confidence. He had to be coaxed out of bed and grew increasingly withdrawn. One of the few people he would talk to was me, whom he called several times a day complaining of this pain or that. I took him to doctors and a psychiatrist, but the doctors were not helpful, and he hated the psychiatrist. I felt harassed, angry, helpless, and rejected. My mother had been very disabled by the end of her life, but I could always make her happy, or so she led me to believe. My father, on the other hand, would not grace me with a smile.

"My father is ruining my life," I kept repeating to Dan. He tried to help by making practical suggestions and taking my father out every Friday afternoon. But when I continued to brood, Dan, a former rehabilitation doctor, decided to treat me as one of his patients with chronic pain. My father's situation was not improving, so I had better learn to accept it and cope. When I would complain about my dad, Dan would change the subject. This infuriated me. How could he be so insensitive and unsympathetic? But gradually, I saw the wisdom of his ways. My life on the whole was rich and good, and he was trying to restore me to a more balanced outlook.

Then, one morning, two winters ago, I got a call from the emergency room of the local hospital. My father had called an ambulance earlier that morning complaining of stomach pains. The hospital doctors had examined him carefully but found nothing amiss, aside from mild constipation. When I got to the hospital to pick him up, I found my father sitting in the emergency room in his ragged pajamas—his thin, wispy hair unkempt. He had no shoes, no wallet, no glasses. I got him into the car and began to drive away before I gave vent to my anger. When we got back to his house, I discovered he had no key, so I called the office of the retirement home. A staff member arrived with a key and escorted my father carefully into the house. "He can walk by himself," I grumbled to the man, feeling miserable at my own meanness. After I had checked to make sure that my father was settled back in his home, I began a hasty retreat. "Is today your birthday?" my father asked. When I told him that it was the next day, he said, "Well, have a good birthday then."

Two weeks later, on the eve of my sister's birthday, I got an email at work from the head nurse at the retirement village. "Your father refused to get out of bed this morning and then threatened suicide," she wrote. I knew my father wasn't about to kill himself—he is prone to temperamental outbursts and dramatic displays—but his reaction was a call for help, and I did not have the skills or experience to handle my father's distress. The nurse suggested that I hire a woman named Joanne to be a "geriatric case manager." Joanne turned out to be very competent, knowledgeable, and proactive. She freed me from being my father's nurse so that I could become his daughter again.

Despite a variety of medications, my father remains depressed. But his anger has dissipated and so has mine. I have begun to look forward to visits with my dad. I always come with a milkshake (he weighs only 115 pounds) and an agenda. Sometimes, I bring an art book so we can look over the glossy pictures together. Other times, I bring a jigsaw puzzle with very large pieces. As I watch my father struggle to understand the puzzle shapes or manipulate them with his trembling hands, I wonder how many times one can grieve for a parent and chide myself for the days that I was too busy or could not bring myself to see him. But things are not so bad. We often sit close together on his sofa, listening to Bach violin partitas while reading along with the musical score. My father lifts his hand and conducts, seeming to draw the notes right out of thin air. Such moments are filled with tenderness and grace. "I love you very much," I say to my father as I kiss him good-bye.

"I love you very much, too," he responds, and we are both at peace.

I sent this memory to Oliver because it was inspired by his book, and he found it deeply moving.

One Moment in Time

On the evening of November 9, 2010, Oliver hosted a publication party for *The Mind's Eye* and invited his usual New York friends (writers, neurologists, the music therapist with whom he worked closely, his physical therapist, his piano teacher, fellow fern lovers, and more). Kate asked me if I, as one of the subjects in his book, would say a few words, and I agreed.

I took the train into Manhattan early in the day and spent my time walking around Greenwich Village and Tribeca while repeatedly reciting my little speech to myself. When, at the party, my turn to speak came, I recited from memory:

In 2002, I experienced a remarkable change in my vision. I had been cross-eyed and stereoblind all my life but, at the age of 48, through optometric vision therapy, I learned to coordinate my eyes and see in 3D. The world appeared deeper, wider, more textured and detailed, and I could see the pockets of space between things. I was overjoyed but also very hesitant to tell others about it. Why? Because for a half century, there was a dogma that stereovision must develop during a critical period in early childhood or it could never develop. I was afraid that if I told my story to scientists and physicians, they would judge my experience, which to me was so profound, joyful, and revelatory, as impossible—I must be crazy, naive, or at least prone to exaggeration.

So I kept quiet for about three years, but then one night in late December 2004, I felt like I was going to burst and, in one long exhale, I wrote a very lengthy letter to Oliver. I didn't really know Oliver at the time, nor did I know he loved stereoscopy, but I had read his books, and if I took him at his word, then I thought maybe he would listen to me as he listened to his patients. Oliver did read my letter and wrote back, asking to come visit.

What to do now? Oliver Sacks was coming to study me, so I had better study Oliver. I reread his books, trying to figure out the man, and more immediately, since he was going to be my guest, I tried to find out what he liked and disliked. So when he came, I took him swimming and fed him his favorite foods, including brown, overripe bananas.

Oliver came armed with stereo devices and gadgets to test my 3D vision. Although I didn't think of it at the time, Oliver wanted to know more than how good my vision was. He wanted to see how I reacted to seeing in 3D, to how this change had impacted my sense of myself in the greater world. He was probing and curious but always gentle and often funny. He never objectified or patronized. In this way, he was able to get to the essence of my and other people's stories, as is evident when you read *The Mind's Eye* and his other books.

Over the last five years, our relationship has changed from that of writer and subject to friends. Oliver is also a wonderful teacher and mentor. In fact, Oliver, I think of you as my Uncle Tungsten, just like you are an Uncle Tungsten to many other people, including devoted readers that you've never met.

So congratulations on another wonderful book, and I look forward to what comes next.

Uncle Tungsten was the nickname for Oliver's favorite uncle. He introduced Oliver to chemistry, inspiring Oliver to title his childhood memoir *Uncle Tungsten: Memories of a Chemical Boyhood.* When, toward the end of my speech, I had mentioned that Oliver was my Uncle Tungsten, I heard someone sigh, and when I finished speaking, I looked around and saw Oliver. He was looking directly at me with wide open eyes.

There are moments, though rare they may be, when all the stars and planets in one's personal universe align. This was one of those moments. I had said "thank you" out loud.

Pet Rock

Oliver was off to a book reading in Philadelphia the next day, but I left in his office a special gift, a beautiful "pet rock," and this rock wrote letters, too.

November 9, 2010

Dear Oliver,

Let me introduce myself. I am a member of the Monson Gneiss, a proud family with a long, distinguished, and earth-shaking history. We first emerged during the Ordovician as island arcs from a subduction zone under the Iapetus Ocean off the coast of Laurentia, a proto–North America. Then, during the Acadian orogeny starting 380 million years ago, in a spectacular collision of land masses, we melted and reemerged as the beautifully banded gneiss we are today. For some time now, I have been sunning myself by the shores of the Quabbin Reservoir until a few weeks ago, when Stereo Sue picked me up and put me in her knapsack. She told me that she is taking me to you, a doctor in Greenwich Village, who writes about his patients and other people. This made me happy. I am favorably inclined toward members of this very young species, for they move on top of us with remarkable speed and lightness, exclaiming all the while about our beautiful swirls and racing stripes.

If you use me as a doorstop, I will take note of every person and spider who walks by. If you use me as a paperweight, I will read what I am guarding. If you put me on a shelf with your favorite metals, then I will forge bonds of friendship, for I am composed of plagioclase, quartz, and biotite: sodium, calcium, aluminum, silicon, oxygen, potassium, iron, and magnesium.

Yes—I very much look forward to my new home. Indeed, with a patience far greater than that of a Galápagos tortoise or bristlecone pine, I have anticipated this event for a few hundred million years.

Yours from the ground up,

Monson B. Gneiss

The reply came typed on paper from a yellow legal pad.

November 11, 2010

Dear Sue,

. . .

Getting back from Philadelphia today I found the enchanting letter from your friend Mr. Gneiss—do thank him for me—and then Mr. Gneiss himself, with the beautiful contours he mentions. But what he did not mention—perhaps he was too modest—was the fact that he had a <u>pentagonal</u> symmetry, and such a symmetry is impossible, not allowed, in crystallography. Cubic, hexagonal lattice, yes—but not

pentagonal. So he has a supramolecular symmetry, Is a
"quasi-crystal"—at least I think so, the whole subject (which
engaged Linus Pauling, among others, in his final years) is
beyond me.*

. . .

Forgive this awful typing and yellow paper—but wanted
to write to you straightaway,

Love, Oliver

A month later, when in Manhattan, I gave Oliver a small mystery
mineral, challenging him to figure out what it was. Oliver looked
nervous at first, examined it minutely, but then relaxed, smiled,
walked over to his apartment entryway, and stuck the mineral to the
metal door. My mystery mineral was magnetite.

* For a delightful account of the discovery of quasi-crystals, read *The Second Kind of
Impossible* by Paul J. Steinhardt.

Experimentum suitatis

Four months later, on March 17, 2011, Oliver tripped in his office and broke his hip. So, he was back in the hospital for more surgery, but the hospital stay hardly slowed him down. While there, he took careful notes on the effects of his spinal anesthesia, wrote another several hundred words for his new book *Hallucinations*, and did an interview for *Rolling Stone*. I sent him several windup toys that I found online in a retro toy store. He was particularly fond of the stegosaurus, whose labored, lumbering gait reminded him of his own.

> Thank you so much for your warm letter, and all the puzzles and toys—mechanical and verbal—you enclosed. They were my solace in my first days here back from the hospital—tho' I have now got into a writing jig which will sustain me in these somewhat frustrating postoperative weeks, when I cannot swim, or go to the gym, or walk <u>alone</u>.
>
> . . .
>
> My mother died in her 78th year, and I have had a certain superstitious apprehension about mine. Hopefully the Fates will be satisfied with a broken hip.

Oliver was not the only one who broke bones. On November 22, 2011, I slipped while walking down a muddy hillside and broke the radius bone in my right arm. Following Oliver's lead, I decided to treat my broken arm and the recovery process as a scientific study with me as my own experimental subject.

On the day I broke my arm, I bought a composition book, the type with a black-and-white cover that schoolchildren use, and started my broken arm journal. My injury affected much more than the radius bone. And so, five days after the break, I wrote, "I feel like a wounded animal. Just like the cast hides and protects my arm, I feel like hiding myself. I feel different. I smell different. I get chilled and nauseated."

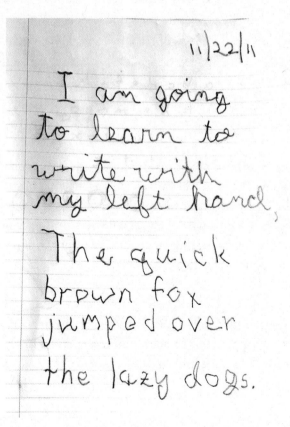

I was strongly right-handed and now had to write with my left, non-dominant hand so that the journal served as a way to track my left-hand-writing progress. I found writing cursive to be easier than writing print. When examining my left-handed-formed letters under a dissecting microscope, I discovered that curves, like in the letter S, were really made up of several short line segments and wondered if drawing a smooth curve required precisely timed recruitment of motor neurons and their muscle fibers.

While visiting my father in the nursing home, a kind physical therapist gave me elastic laces to secure my sneakers. Slicing carrots was difficult not only because I could not direct the knife well with my left hand but because I could not hold the carrot stable with my right. But eleven days after the break, I wrote, "I feel like I made a leap with my left hand today. Writing is faster, and the hairbrush feels more natural in my left hand. What is this 'natural' feeling?"

A month later, while my arm was still in a cast, I visited Oliver and brought my notebook of left-handed writing with me. He studied it with interest. I told him that I had trouble using my left hand to draw a five-pointed star, so he tried drawing the star, too, with his left hand but had no trouble doing this.

A few weeks later, my cast was removed, I underwent hand therapy, and on February 6, 2012, wrote to Oliver all about it. Almost all my past letters had been typed, but not this one.

Feb. 6, 2012

Dear Oliver,

    I am beginning this
letter by writing with my
left (non-dominant) hand.
I've been writing with it
since November 22 when
I fell and broke the
radius bone in my right
arm. Although my
left-handed penmanship
is wobbly and child-like,
I like writing this way.
I am forced to write
more slowly which also
slows down my thoughts
and relaxes me. Last week,
I was in Madrid for the
presentation of the Spanish
                         →

version of my book
(Ver en Estereo). It was a
good thing I mastered a
left-handed signature
because I signed a lot of
books, and I couldn't have
done that yet with my
right hand.

After I broke my arm,
it was casted for six weeks,
and, during that time, the
radius bone mended
itself. But it didn't heal
quite right. The radius
bone and the wrist bones
above it are no longer
in perfect alignment.
The hand surgeon
recommended surgery, but

③

Dan thought otherwise.
The surgeon agreed
that I could try rehab
first and elect surgery
later if the therapy wasn't
helpful.

   I really enjoy my
twice-a-week hand therapy
sessions. Sometimes, my
forearm and hand are
plunged into hot wax
and then baked between
hot towels to loosen up
the scar tissue. Ah-that
feels good! This is
followed by massage
and exercises.

   (My hand therapist
insists that I use my

(4)

right hand for writing as much as possible so I'll switch now to writing with my right hand.)

I find working with physical therapists, occupational therapists, and vision therapists to be a bit unnerving because they can see right through me. I can't hide. When the hand therapist first asked me to bend my wrist in various directions, it was as if she asked me to bend my knee the wrong way. It took great effort and involved not just my arm but my whole body and physiology, and the therapist noticed this right

(5)

away. During the first session, when I was grinding away at a supination - pronation exercise, the therapist told me to stop. "Why?" I asked because I hadn't completed the requisite number of repetitions.

"Because you've stopped breathing, your left eyelid is drooping, and the nystagmus in your eyes has really increased."

I was aware of the nystagmus because my view had become jittery. This nystagmus called "fixation nystagmus" or "manifest latent nystagmus" is present in people with infantile esotropia but is usually quite damped. I notice it from

(6)

time to time, but it is rare for
anyone else to see it or comment
on it.

It did not surprise me
though that the therapy exercises
produced such whole-body effects.
When I did challenging fusion
exercises in vision therapy, I
would sometimes feel queasy,
break out in a sweat, and
develop a tremor in my hands.
If these reactions were strong,
I'd back off, but if these
effects were mild, I'd push
through them. I took them as a
sign that I was putting my
eyes in new positions relative
to each other and learning new
spatial interpretations.

Anyway, I've been practicing

⑦

my wrist exercises and just saw
the hand surgeon. He agreed that
the therapy is working. I may
never recover full range of motion
in the wrist, but I'll be able
to do everything I'd like to do
with it. Just a few days ago,
I began playing the piano again.
My fingers and wrist felt
stiff, but with practice, I was
able to play, with both hands,
Bach's Two Part Invention #10.
I played it under tempo
but fluidly. That was a real
'shot in the arm'!

      I hope you, your new
book, Kate, and Hailey are
all happy and well.
          Love,
                Stereo Sue

February 6, 2012

Dear Oliver,

I am beginning this letter using my left (non-dominant) hand. I've been writing with it since November 22 when I fell and broke the radius bone in my right arm. Although my left-handed penmanship is wobbly and childlike, I like writing this way. I am forced to write more slowly which also slows down my thoughts and relaxes me. Last week I was in Madrid for the presentation of the Spanish version of my book (<u>Ver en Estéreo</u>). It was a good thing I mastered a left-handed signature because I signed a lot of books, and I couldn't have done that yet with my right hand.

After I broke my arm, it was casted for six weeks, and, during that time, the radius bone mended itself. But it didn't heal quite right. The radius bone and the wrist bones above it are no longer in perfect alignment. The hand surgeon recommended surgery, but Dan [a rehab doc] thought otherwise. The surgeon agreed that I could try rehab first and elect surgery later if the therapy wasn't helpful.

I really enjoy my twice-a-week hand therapy sessions. Sometimes, my forearm and hand are plunged into hot wax and then baked between hot towels to loosen up the scar tissue. Ah—that feels good! This is followed by massage and exercises.

(My hand therapist insists that I use my right hand for writing as much as possible so I'll switch now to writing with my right hand.)

I find working with physical therapists, occupational therapists, or vision therapists to be a bit unnerving because they see right through me. I can't hide. When the hand therapist first asked me to bend my wrist in various directions, it was as if she had asked me to bend my knee the wrong way. It took great effort and involved not just my arm but my whole body and physiology, and the therapist noticed this right away. During the first session, when I was grinding away at a supination-pronation exercise, the therapist told me to stop. "Why?" I asked because I hadn't completed the requisite number of repetitions.

"Because you've stopped breathing, your left eyelid is drooping, and the nystagmus[*] in your eyes has really increased."

I was aware of the nystagmus because my view had become jittery. This nystagmus, called "fixation nystagmus" or "manifest latent nystagmus," is present in people with infantile esotropia but is usually quite damped. I notice it from time to time, but it is rare for anyone else to see it or comment on it.

It did not surprise me though that the therapy exercises produced such whole-body effects. When I did challenging fusion exercises in vision therapy, I would often feel queasy, break out in a sweat, and develop a tremor in my hands. If these reactions were strong, I'd back off, but if these effects were mild, I'd push through them. I took them as a sign that I was putting my eyes in new positions relative to each other and learning new spatial interpretations.

Anyway, I've been practicing my hand exercises and just saw the hand surgeon. He agreed that the therapy is working. I may never recover full range of motion in the wrist, but I'll be able to do everything I'd like to do with it. Just a few days ago, I began playing the piano again. My fingers and wrist felt stiff, but, with practice, I was able to play, with two hands, Bach's Two Part Invention #10. I played it under

---

[*] Nystagmus is an involuntary back-and-forth movement of the eyes and can occur in people who have infantile esotropia or have been cross-eyed since the first six months of life.

tempo but fluidly. That was a real "shot in the arm"!

I hope you, your new book, Kate, and Hailey are all happy and well.

Love,

Stereo Sue

My letter revived a discussion of rehabilitation that began when Oliver underwent knee replacement surgery three years earlier, which in turn was, for Oliver, a continuation of thoughts triggered by a knee operation in 1974 as discussed in his book *A Leg to Stand On.*

OLIVER SACKS, M.D.

2 HORATIO ST. #3G · NEW YORK, NY · 10014
TEL: 212.633.8373 · FAX: 212.633.8928
MAIL@OLIVERSACKS.COM   2/24/12

Dear Sue,

A belated "Thank You" for your fine left-handed letter of the 6th. I think it very impressive to write this well when one has never written before with one's non-dominant hand. But it sounds as if your normally bimanual activities (at piano and computer) have remained fluent. When I had to use my left hand (after shoulder surgery on the right side) in 2003 I was able to do quite rapid 1-finger-"hunt-and-peck," tho' my handwriting was "wobbly and childlike" (to use your words). How is the arm now? Was it in a sling? If not, did you find yourself "sparing" or "neglecting" the entire arm (and shoulder), even tho' the fracture was at the tip of the radius?

I think it's difficult to know if <u>a bit</u> of misalignment matters. You are probably doing wisely to test and see, rather than running into any premature, and perhaps unnecessary, surgery.

I was <u>most</u> interested by the especial difficulties (and autonomic and other upsets) you ran into when asked to bend the wrist this way and that—was bending the wrist after its immobilization painful, or (just!) in some broader sense (slow to) unimaginable or undoable? (I think of the problem with my leg after surgery). Some of the difficulties are the brain's reaction to (what Luria called the "cerebral resonances") of a peripheral injury or disorder. Maybe you should add Arpeggios to 2-part inventions.

. . .

March 17, 2012

Dear Oliver,

In your last letter, you asked a question that I have been thinking a lot about. You wondered if the difficulties I had first bending my wrist after a radius bone fracture resulted from the pain involved or from a deeper inhibition by the brain. Did the wrist bending seem impossible or unimaginable?

Certainly, there was a strong autonomic reaction to bending my wrist. When I first tried to do the exercises, I felt queasy and light-headed even though my hand therapist had heated, stretched, and massaged my arm beforehand. As I was grinding away at the exercises, she watched me carefully, reminding me to breathe. She told me that patients sometimes faint from the exercises but, upon seeing my shocked look, added that she had not had a patient faint in her office for five years.

I noticed that the exercises were easier to do in some body positions than others. I could, for example, pronate and supinate my right wrist most easily when my arms were hanging down by my sides. To do the same exercises with the right arm bent at the elbow was more difficult, and to do the exercises with the arm bent and the fist clenched was harder still. So, at home, I gradually progressed by doing the exercises in the more permissive and then more difficult positions. The therapist encouraged me (essentially gave me permission) to incorporate these movements into everyday tasks. I found the best tasks involved water. I would practice the wrist movements while swimming or engage in them quite naturally while washing dishes or wringing out clothes. Just this week, for the first time in four months, I could use my right hand to turn the key in the car ignition.

With wrist extension, I decided to take advantage of a primitive reflex. I would work on wrist extension while activating the asymmetric tonic neck reflex—that is, I would extend my right arm to the right, rotate my head so it was looking at my right hand, and flex my left side. Under these conditions, I felt less resistance to right wrist extension. (If I tried the same exercise on the left side, I did not find the reflex to help with left wrist extension, but then again, I had no problem extending the left wrist.)

My hand therapy allowed me to regain functions that I had only recently lost and *could* imagine regaining. Except in one instance, I had not lost my sense of connection with my arm and wrist. So, unlike you with your leg, I could imagine what it felt like to move my wrist. I did not believe that the wrist movements were impossible—just frightening to do because they might cause pain or damage.

The one unusual instance occurred when, after three weeks, my first cast was removed, the arm briefly examined, and a new

cast put on. When the first cast came off, I momentarily
panicked. I did not know where my arm was in space or how to
move it. The man who puts on and removes casts seemed
familiar with this reaction and immediately suggested that I use
my left arm to nestle and support the right.

With vision therapy, I had to develop new ways of using
my eyes, and, here, I did feel at times that the tasks set
before me were undoable and unimaginable. The
breakthrough came when I first *felt* my eyes turn in and turn
out together while fixating beads at different distances along
the Brock string. That moment, which occurred now ten
years ago, remains so vivid that I still recall it in great detail.
It was right after this experience with the Brock string that I
went out to my car and saw the steering wheel floating
before me. You write in your *Leg* book that acting is the key
to all therapy. For me, this statement rings very true. I would
not have experienced any perceptual changes without a
change in my actions.

One young man from Great Britain, an esotrope* like me,
told me an interesting story. He was doing vision therapy
while also attending school and preparing for some
important exams. He had developed the ability to see in
stereo depth while working with polarized vectograms in the
optometrist's office,† but he could not see any stereo depth
outside in the real world. He felt that he was inhibiting
himself. Some part of himself would not let him see in stereo
because it would be distracting and disorienting and might
compromise his ability to do well on his exams. When the
school term ended, he went home to his childhood farm, and

---

* Esotrope refers to a person with crossed eyes.

† When looking at polarized vectograms while wearing polarized lenses, each eye sees a
slightly different image which, if fused in the brain, is seen as a single image floating in
space. In a similar way, we experience a 3D effect when wearing polarized lenses while
watching a 3D movie.

while taking a relaxing walk around the fields, the world emerged in 3D.

Another strabismic individual told me that, while doing vision therapy, he found ways "to put himself into stereo." He would use certain behaviors to trigger the onset of his stereovision. These stories make me wonder if turning on stereovision, like your experience of learning, via Mendelssohn, to walk again, requires switching to a different brain state.[*] And that state, so different from the state you may currently be in, may seem undoable or impossible. The key is to find a way to flip the switch and then to remember what it feels like to act in this new way. The Brock string may have done for me what Mendelssohn's music did for you— woke up and organized latent circuits that orchestrated movements that seemed unimaginable, yet, were as natural as can be.

Love,
Stereo Sue

Shortly after this letter exchange, on March 20, 2012, I was in Manhattan and visited Oliver. While standing in his kitchen, waiting for the tea water to boil, Oliver told me to write about rehabilitation. He felt that he had not given enough attention to the rehabilitation process when he wrote about his recovery from a leg injury in *A Leg to Stand On*. "Now that *Fixing My Gaze* is done, it's time to write some more," he insisted. In Oliver's mind, there was no resting on one's laurels.

---

[*] In *A Leg to Stand On*, Oliver describes a leg injury from which he had to learn to walk again. He was able to regain the rhythm and coordination of walking when he heard Mendelssohn's violin concerto in E minor playing in his head.

Musical Interlude III

In 2013, I hardly wrote to Oliver at all except for a heartfelt letter celebrating his eightieth birthday. As the year drew to a close, however, I sent a long newsy letter that began,

> December 29, 2013 (It's really the 26th, but I've dated this letter with the 29th because the first letter I sent to you was dated December 29, 2004.)
>
> Dear Oliver,
>
> This is just a letter to wish you a very happy new year full of good health and good writing. I've just finished a busy semester of teaching, which always generates new stories. Ever since you published *Musicophilia* in 2007, I've asked the students in my "Art, Music, and the Brain" class to read your book and to keep a two-day diary of all their musical imagery. In the past, the students have come to class with long lists of songs, quite surprised by how much and how often music played in their heads. We've had fun figuring out why certain songs came to mind and where and how this imagery was created in the brain.
>
> But this year was different—

The students arrived in class with very few entries in their diaries and admitted rather sheepishly that very few songs had popped into their heads. They simply had no time for musical imagery because they were always hooked up to their iPods or smartphones, even when going to sleep. Their minds were rarely free to wander, untouched by outside music or other interference. This was a big change even from one year ago.

Only one student took exception to this general trend, though she, too, experienced little musical imagery. This student grew up in China, where she had been tutored from early childhood in Zen meditation. She did not own an iPod or a smartphone; thus, when not otherwise engaged, she quieted her mind. After class, she told me that she wished she could experience more musical imagery; I told her that I wished I could quiet my mind.

On most days, I walk to and from work, a round trip of four miles, often listening to my iPod. But, after talking with my students, I put the iPod away. Instead, I try an exercise that an orchestra conductor once described to me when I asked him how he could simultaneously keep track of so many instruments. He told me that on days when he was not at his peak, he'd walk around the streets of New York City listening to all the sounds he could hear at once. So I do the same thing now, only in my more rural habitat.

OLIVER SACKS, M.D.   Jan 4/14

2 HORATIO ST. #3G · NEW YORK, NY · 10014
TEL: 212.633.8373 · FAX: 212.633.8928
MAIL@OLIVERSACKS.COM

Dear Sue,

Thanks for your splendid letter of Dec 26/29—your letters are infrequent but so rich, like banquets. I can hardly believe it is <u>nine</u> years since your original letter (or, a much grimmer association, <u>eight</u> years since my melanoma was diagnosed in Dec '05).

. . .

I am intrigued (and disquieted) by your observations that (most of) your students experienced (voluntary or involuntary) musical imagery in 2007, but now, continuously hooked up to their iPods or smartphones, no longer do so, are totally absorbed in their electronic music (or speech or texting). That, in effect, they have no internal privacy, no unoccupied inner space, where the 'default network' of the brain would be free (to imagine or introspect). I am very conscious—how can one not be in a place like New York?—of <u>social</u> breakdown produced by these devices—in effect blindness and deafness to the wearers' human (and physical) environments—but what you say makes it sound as if these "wired" people are equally deaf or blind to <u>themselves</u>, are getting cut off not only from those around them, but from themselves.

I, too, was troubled by my students' reports. In the next year, I told them to unhook themselves from their devices for two days so that they could experience musical imagery. They found this novel and intriguing, though they missed their devices and wired themselves up as soon as the assignment was completed.

My end-of-2013 letter also included a story about my father, who, at this time, lived in a nearby nursing home and was so depressed he never voluntarily got out of bed.

> Although my father often seems distant and unengaged, I experienced a great moment with him recently, and, not surprisingly, music was involved. My brother had come to visit, and we had talked at my father for some time without getting much of a response from him. So I started humming the beginning of Beethoven's Razumovsky Quartet (op. 59, no. 1, in F major). When my siblings and I were growing up, my father played regularly with chamber music groups and practiced almost every evening, using Music Minus One records.[*] So this quartet was very familiar to me and my brother; it was in our bones. My brother joined my singing, and we sang (as you would write) with great brio. As the music rose in pitch and volume, so did our voices. We reached a great crescendo but then both stopped abruptly, not sure exactly of the next pitch. My brother and I cracked up and so did my dad—not with a mild-mannered chuckle but with a face-transforming, tears-in-the-eyes guffaw. We had reached him! I keep recalling that moment. It made me happy for more than a week.

To this, Oliver wrote in his letter of January 11, 2014,

> I was, at once, saddened, puzzled, then very moved (with a sort of "Hoorah!" feeling) at your description of your father's remoteness, and his sudden return to himself in a shared laugh or a sudden, shared musical uncertainty.

---

[*] My father's Music Minus One records featured world-class musicians playing quartets and quintets, but the first violinist was absent. My father then played the record while filling in the first violin part.

Bioelectricity

My December 29, 2013, letter also described an article that excited me but was not about music. It was about plants—their senses, behavior, and defenses. This was just the sort of information that Oliver loved.

> Did you see the article by Michael Pollan on plants in the December 23 issue of *The New Yorker*?* It's a great piece and one that I'll have my introductory biology students read for sure. Pollan writes that many of us view plants as passive, as "the mute, immobile furniture of our world," in part because (and this reminded me of your article "Speed") plants conduct their lives in a slower time frame. I always knew that plants can regenerate from small bits of themselves, but Pollan points out that this trait is necessary if your parts are constantly getting eaten. Caffeine in the nectar of coffee plants may not only serve as a chemical defense but may also help the pollinating bees remember the plant better! He elaborates on the way plants communicate via underground mycorrhizal networks (I love that!), describes their sophisticated sensory capabilities (they have fifteen

---

* Michael Pollan, "The Intelligent Plant," *The New Yorker*, December 23, 2013.

to twenty distinct senses), and then asks how a brainless organism can integrate all that information. This is where some scientists talk about plant intelligence, and other scientists freak out. He discusses how *Mimosa pudica*, the sensitive plant that folds its leaves when touched, can habituate to a repetitive but harmless stimulus. This should not be so surprising because it's not the first observation of habituation in a nerve-less organism. I have my students read an excerpt from H. S. Jennings's wonderful 1906 book, *Behavior of the Lower Organisms*, in which Jennings describes habituation in the single-celled *Stentor*.*

Clearly, with this topic, I hit a nerve. Oliver, at the time, was revising an article that eventually was titled "The Mental Life of Plants and Worms, Among Others" and was published in the April 24, 2014, issue of *The New York Review of Books*. In his letter of January 4, 2014, he discussed Pollan's article:

> I thought it very good, and <u>balanced</u> (in an area where people may go overboard), and I have filed it with my much-read and admired copy of Daniel Chamovitz's book (<u>What a Plant Knows</u>). I have and love Jennings' (1906) book—at least a (Kessinger) reprint of it, not least Chapter 10 in which he describes habituation <u>and</u> sensitization in <u>Stentor</u> and <u>Vorticella</u> (I have tender memories of these from my biology days).
>
> Your speaking of these—they have both been very much in my mind these last few days—confronts me with a dilemma. I have, as you know, been fiddling with an essay

---

* Habituation is a simple form of learning that involves the organism's response to a repetitive stimulus. When the stimulus is first applied, the organism may give a strong response. If the stimulus turns out to be harmless, then the organism may respond less forcefully or habituate to further applications of the stimulus. Thus, Jennings stimulated *Stentor*, a single-celled pond water organism, with a gentle jet of water, causing the microorganism to contract. After the first jet, *Stentor* reacted much less forcefully to the stimulus.

(provisionally <u>In Praise of Invertebrates</u>) since I first drafted
it (in the summer of 2012, when I was away at Blue Mountain
Center). The original (and still current) piece/plan was to
<u>contrast</u> animals and plants—plants as rooted, having to
be elaborately programmed (large genomes!) for all their
"devices" (Darwin's term), including trigger hairs of <u>Dionaea</u>[*]
and "tentacles" of <u>Drosera</u>,[†] as well as the apical gravity,
light sensors etc in root apex: contrasting these, then, with
animals which are (generally) mobile, move about a complex,
changeable world, have sensory and motor equipment of
some sophistication, and nervous system (with <u>synapses</u>)
to allow forms of memory and learning. I exemplify this
on a rising "scale" of jellyfish, earthworms, <u>Aplysia</u>, insects
to <u>cephalopods</u>. . . . But how do I accommodate plants and
micro-organisms without sacrificing my original nice, simple
plant/animal dichotomy? (Of course the piece is essentially
about <u>continuity</u>, and I quote Darwin's letter to Asa Gray
when he speaks of <u>Drosera</u> as "not only a wonderful plant,
but a most sagacious animal.")

    <u>Stentor</u> etc I can easily embody in a footnote—but
plants?! I'll figure a way.

Venus flytraps and sundews trap and digest insects, while *Stentor*
modifies its behavior or habituates when presented repeatedly with
the same irritating stimulus. How can plants, such as the Venus
flytrap or sundew, or, for that matter, single-celled protists such as
Stentor, behave in such animal-like ways? Neither plants nor protists have nervous systems like we animals do. But nervous systems
did not arise out of a vacuum—they co-opted whatever mechanisms
worked well for signaling from one cell to another. And one great
way to turn on, off, or send signals is through ion channels. One can

---

* *Dionaea* is the genus name for the Venus flytrap, a carnivorous plant.
† *Drosera* is the genus name for sundews, which are carnivorous plants.

think of an ion channel as a tunnel in the cell membrane that can open and close and when open lets specific ions, such as calcium, sodium, potassium, or chloride, through the membrane. The nerve impulse or action potential results from movements of ions through these channels. Plants and protists have ion channels, too. I had studied ion channels in non-animals and now proposed a possible solution to Oliver's dilemma in my next letter.

Jan. 19, 2014

Dear Oliver,

After reading your letter of Jan. 11, I picked up a copy of *What a Plant Knows* and really enjoyed it. I didn't know that plants could be so sensitive to touch and emit volatile gases like methyl salicylate that signal other leaves of impending attack. Nor have I thought much about electrical signaling in plants and algae. But Chamovitz's book reminded me that, during my first year at Mount Holyoke, I taught a lab in which students recorded action potentials from the green alga *Chara*. *Chara*'s cells are enormous, which make for easy microelectrode recordings, although the cell walls are a bit difficult to penetrate. The depolarizing phase of *Chara*'s action potentials result from calcium influx, which lead to activation of calcium-dependent chloride channels and a large chloride efflux. What struck me most about these action potentials was not the unusual ion currents underlying them but their super long time course. *Chara*'s action potentials lasted several seconds, and once a cell fired, it could not generate another action potential for more than a minute!

In nature, *Chara* cells fire action potentials when the cell membrane is deformed. The resulting influx of calcium causes a cessation of cytoplasmic streaming, which may prevent leakage of cytoplasm through a pierced or leaky membrane. In *Mimosa pudica*, calcium action potentials cause the leaves to fold, in *Dionaea*, they cause the lobes to snap shut, and in paramecia, calcium action potentials trigger ciliary reversal. Perhaps, the original function of action potentials in eukaryotes was not for rapid and long-distance signaling but rather to provide a mechanism to inject a bolus of calcium into a particular region of the cell. Then calcium could trigger all sorts of other changes, even primitive forms of learning.

. . .

However, high levels of calcium are toxic, which limits how often a cell can generate calcium currents and calcium action potentials. Hence, the use of action potentials for rapid and repetitive signaling and for nervous systems had to wait for the emergence of a channel that was selective for a less toxic ion. So along came the voltage-gated sodium channel, which probably evolved from duplication and mutation of a calcium channel gene.

Sodium channels have a second great advantage over calcium channels in electrical signaling—they turn themselves off. The channels open and then inactivate so rapidly that a nerve cell membrane can recover from an action potential and generate a new one several hundred times per second. This is nothing like the slow-motion action potentials that my students and I saw in *Chara*.

An action potential in *Chara*, *Mimosa pudica*, or *Dionaea* can act like an on switch, registering whether or not a stimulus has occurred and eliciting a response, but that stimulus-response coupling can't be repeated at high rates. Once the lobes of a Venus flytrap shut, for example, it takes a long time for them to open again. But, when cells can fire at a wide range of frequencies, much more information can be coded in the

frequency, firing patterns, and spatial distribution of the
spikes. And when excitable cells, with a wide range of firing
frequencies, connect with one another, they can produce
highly sensitive and coordinated sensorimotor systems.

. . .

All these thoughts increased my appreciation for our
hardworking, self-inactivating sodium channels (and for the
sodium potassium pump!) and made me wonder whether or
not the ancestral, voltage-gated sodium channel also
inactivated itself. I found some papers (see enclosed) on the
evolution of sodium channels, and, sure enough, the
ancestral sodium channel probably had both an activation
and inactivation gate! In fact, the first sodium channels
probably arose, not in animals, but in the common ancestor
of animals and choanoflagellates. Intriguingly, these single-
celled protists also contain a lot of other molecular
machinery, such as cell adhesion and calcium-binding
proteins, which are also used by animals.

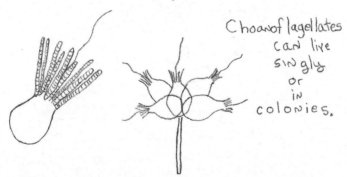

Choanoflagellates
can live
singly
or
in
colonies.

So that's where reading Chamovitz's book took me.

. . .

Yours in every sense,

Stereo Sue

OLIVER SACKS, M.D.   1/27/14

2 HORATIO ST. #3G · NEW YORK, NY · 10014
TEL: 212.633.8373 · FAX: 212.633.8928
MAIL@OLIVERSACKS.COM

Just got back from (a very good trip to) England to find your fabulous letter.

It has answered all my questions—including unspoken ones—and (I think) given me the (ion channel etc) level at which one can bring animals, plants and protozoa together. I found especially exciting your thoughts on how slow (calcium-mediated) cellular transmission might evolve (with development of sodium and potassium channels) into rapidly propagated (and repeatable) action potentials.

. . .

Again, thanks a 10^6,

and love, Oliver

War and Peace

After watching a 1996 video of pond water microorganisms titled "Predatory Tactics," by Jeremy and Julianne Pickett-Heaps, I knew Oliver would love it. So I sent the tape to him and wrote on March 18, 2014, "You'll see your beloved *Stentor* and other ciliates as well as rotifers, beautiful *Bryozoa*, and two *Noctiluca* (the bioluminescent dinoflagellates we saw in Woods Hole) vying for a poor rotifer. (The rotifer may be one thousand cells big, but it's smaller than the single-celled *Noctiluca*!)"

To this, Oliver responded on June 9, 2014,

Dear Sue,

I have owed you a letter for far too long.

I looked at <u>Predatory Tactics</u> the day it arrived—and was awed by the variety (and often violence, sometimes cunning and patience) of this miniature warfare (like Hobbes' "war of all against all"). I had (sentimentally) portrayed a sort of peaceful, Ediacaran Garden of Eden, rudely and violently ended by the Cambrian*—but, at the <u>micro</u> level, clearly, it was anything but peaceful.

---

* During the Ediacaran period (635 to 541 million years ago), complex multicellular animals developed, but most were soft-bodied and immobile. They may have survived by absorbing nutrients through their skin rather than preying upon each other. During the Cambrian period (541 to 485.4 million years ago), many more predators developed.

I also sent Oliver the astonishing DVD *Microcosmos*, with footage of caterpillars, ants, and other insects as well as *Equisetum* (horse-tails—one of Oliver's favorite plants). "The movie's very French," I wrote, "check out the song accompanying two snails making love." Oliver enjoyed that, too, writing back to me, "Incredible images—made me wonder about the 'ingenuity' of dung beetles using levers, etc., for mechanical advantage, to hoist dung balls over obstacles—Darwin would have loved it!"

Oliver, I sometimes thought, loved Darwin so deeply that he tried to see the world through Darwin's eyes. So did I. In my next letter, dated June 24, 2014, I wrote,

> But in the macro world, I've been watching a more peaceful story unfold. A pair of robins built a nest in the holly bush right outside my study window, and I've watched them work together to prepare and then care for their offspring. Nest building, others say, is instinctual, but this statement is a gross oversimplification. As you've mentioned, animals are problem solvers, and nest building certainly presents a set of problems to be solved. My robins were smart to build their nest in the holly bush right against our house. If our local red-shouldered hawk tried to dive-bomb the nest, he'd crash into the overhanging roof, and the nest and holly are surrounded by bushes on several sides.
>
> I was impressed by the way the robins fed their chicks (and carried the poop away from the nest!), and the way they were always close by, setting off frequent alarm calls. But what really moved me was the way the mother robin brooded over the eggs. Her patient brooding brought me back to an evening a quarter of a century ago, when my son, Andy, had just turned one, and Dan was away at a conference. Late that night, Andy started to have trouble

breathing. Frightened, I called the pediatrician's office and was immediately put through to the doctor on call who explained that Andy had the croup and described what to do. So I spent the rest of the night awake in a rocking chair, holding Andy upright in our tiny bedroom (we lived in Michigan then) with the door closed and the humidifier turned up to the max. I was dripping with sweat, but what I remember most keenly was a feeling—a rare feeling of perfect calmness and clarity. I had no conflicts. There was no place else that I needed to be and nothing else that I needed to do but to hold my baby and listen to him breathe.

We humans have a love-hate relationship with our feelings. On the one hand, we fool ourselves into thinking that we make decisions based on reason and logic. On the other hand, we honor our nobler emotions, such as love and empathy. As I watched the robin sit for hours on her eggs or spread her wings to protect her young during a rainstorm, I wondered if she experienced the same sense of calmness and singleness of purpose that I had during that night when Andy first had the croup. And why not? If strong emotions make me a better parent, wouldn't they also help a robin or any other animal who must put in great effort to nurture their young?

Oliver answered on June 27, 2014,

I am charmed by your (almost Darwinian) description of nest-building and parenting. I would think (but such thinking is always called "sentimental" or "anthropomorphizing")—that that lovely peaceful feeling— which Sherrington calls "consummatory" is known to other animals, at least, birds and mammals.

My cousin Robert John Aumann—you saw/met him at my 80th—founded an Institute for Rationality in

Jerusalem—but "rationality," as he understands/uses the
term takes account of <u>all</u> the emotions, the nobler, and the
not so noble.

Oliver called my description of the robin's behavior "almost
Darwinian." Coming from Oliver, there could hardly be a nicer com-
pliment. Most of Oliver's letter, however, was about his trip to Israel.

Although I had all sorts of apprehensions (and had resisted
a return visit—I was there for several months in 1955–6)
the trip turned out beautifully, especially meeting my now
100-year-old cousin who was practicing medicine and
living independently till she was 98, but is now enjoying
life and (in the last year) has written an autobiography. And
many other cousins—first cousins (all over 90) and their
(innumerable) descendants. Having no <u>direct</u> family now I
feel the cousins, the cousinhood, very important, and had a
lovely sense of welcome, of being embraced by them.

Roaming the Old City was very extraordinary, especially
in the markets—such a mix of Muslims, Jews (of all stripes),
Christians, Arabs, Falasha, Mormon missionaries etc etc—
but there is an uncomfortable tension in the air—so it was a
pleasure, on the last day, to get out of it, drive through the
desert to the Dead Sea (greatly contracted since '55), visit a
Kibbutz with its own Botanical Gardens etc. All
extraordinary. And I survived—my mother had a heart-
attack and died in Israel—and I had a superstitious feeling
that I too would do so—one of my many reasons (tho' so
irrational) for not going there.

All my love, Oliver

A Therapeutic Brain Injury?

At about this time, a surprising turn of events happened with my dad, which I mentioned in an email to Kate and Oliver, dated April 2, 2014:

I had a strange experience yesterday. Due to a cold and travel, I hadn't seen my dad in two weeks. I went to see him yesterday, and the nurses and staff told me that, about 2 weeks ago, he fell and hit the front of his head. Since then, he's been a different man, no longer so depressed and withdrawn but chatty and with a healthy appetite. "What a sweet man," one nurse said to me.

When I saw my dad, he seemed his usual depressed self, but his voice was much stronger, and he looked at me with both eyes instead of turning in his left. He sang with me when I sang him our usual songs. I doubt this change in mood will last long. Over the last 7 years, he spontaneously snapped out of his depression once before, for about a month. Dan describes the fall as a "therapeutic brain injury," which seems a contradiction in terms.

Kate must have shown the email to Oliver because he wrote back to me by physical letter the next day,

> Intriguing story of your father's "therapeutic brain injury."
> All the surgeries (thalamotomies etc.) which used to be
> done for PD* might come in this category, to say nothing of
> lobotomies and ECT†—but, as you say, there can be striking
> spontaneous changes of mood and energy especially in
> PD. And, at least, you can always get him to sing with you.
> The wildest thing in PD is "kinesia paradoxa"‡ (see my long
> footnote pp 10–11 Awakenings).

---

* PD is an abbreviation for Parkinson's disease.
† ECT is an abbreviation for electroconvulsive therapy.
‡ Kinesia paradoxa is the sudden but temporary disappearance of the movement difficulties caused by Parkinson's disease. Some trigger causes the patient to spring into action, to run, for example, when normally they can hardly walk.

Channeling Dad

My father died six months later. On October 29, 2014, I sent an email to Rosalie, Kate, and Oliver.

Dear Rosalie, Kate, and Oliver,

My 92-year-old father began to fail Sunday when his lungs filled with fluid, but his way was eased by morphine. I spent 6 hours with him yesterday. He died at 9 PM.

When my brother Daniel was born (so I was told), my father came home from the hospital and played "Danny Boy" on his violin. When my sister and I were put to bed but would squabble, my father would come into our bedroom with his violin and play us to sleep. He practiced chamber music every night for his weekend string quartet. These were the sounds of my childhood. How much luckier could a girl be?*

Love, Sue

---

* I included an attachment of my father's self-portrait from the 1940s, which is included here as insert photo 5.

OLIVER SACKS, M.D.
2 HORATIO ST. #3G · NEW YORK, NY · 10014
TEL: 212.633.8373 · FAX: 212.633.8928
MAIL@OLIVERSACKS.COM

Nov 7/14

Dear Sue.

 I was "on the road"
(Amsterdam, London, Los Angeles)
for more than two weeks,
and was away when your
letters arrived.

 All my condolences, first,
on your father's passing —
what a gifted, passionate man
he was, if only judging from his
self-portrait — I know how
intensely devoted you were to
him.

Oliver

OLIVER SACKS, M.D.   Nov 7/14

2 HORATIO ST. #3G · NEW YORK, NY · 10014
TEL: 212.633.8373 · FAX: 212.633.8928
MAIL@OLIVERSACKS.COM

I was "on the road" (Amsterdam, London, Los Angeles) for
more than two weeks, and was away when your letters
arrived.

All my condolences, first, on your father's passing. What
a gifted, passionate man he was, if only judging from his
self-portrait. I know how intensely devoted you were to him.

. . .

[signature]

One month later, in December 2014, my family and I went on a
long-planned-for vacation to Aruba. My dad was still very much on
my mind. I thought about the letters he wrote to me as a child, and
this gave me an idea for a letter I would send to Oliver.

December 30, 2014

Dear Oliver,

When I was twelve years old, I spent a month at a
summer camp in western Connecticut. I loved it because we
slept in cabins in the woods, swam in a cold, clear lake, and
sang at the start and end of every meal. After lunch, we had
our daily siesta, during which I wrote letters home. My
father responded in his own style—with missives that
contained no words, just pictures.

Now that my dad has passed away and I'm no longer

occupied with his care, my mind is free to wander, and memories such as my father's picture-letters keep bubbling up. This particular memory inspired me to buy a sketchbook to take with me on our family's vacation last week to Aruba. So I've decided to send you a picture letter of sorts about our trip. (Pictures are xeroxed from my sketchbook.)

Aruba (as you probably know) was formed about 90 million years ago when the southern edge of the Caribbean plate subducted under the South American plate, forcing up lava. There's a lot of quartz diorite on the island, and I collected many pieces with crystals of varying sizes. This poor rock has had a hard life—born first as magma and then metamorphosed underground before finally being extruded to the surface. I've sent you two specimens with crystals of different sizes, which I hope you can see with your magnifying glass.

Dan, Jenny, Andy, and I, as well as Jenny's husband, David, spent the first two days on the island at a little hotel across a busy road from the major hotel strip and beach. I decided to document this time by sketching objects of leisure, such as

Dan's hat:

and a beach chair:

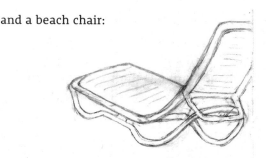

It took me two days to sketch the dumb chair. On three occasions, other vacationers came by and unwittingly moved or sat down in the chair I was using as my model! When I showed an early version of my sketch to David, he remarked that it looked like an "Escher chair." It was easy to see that the perspective was off but not so easy to make it better. I had to pay great attention to the relationship between the different parts and edges in the chair, and in doing so, developed a better sense of how hard it must be for L., my friend who gained sight at age 15, to see the whole chair from its parts. When I was finally satisfied with the way the chair looked, I rounded all the edges to give it a more casual and relaxed appearance.

Our hotel was nestled among palm and mesquite trees and, on the second night, I saw a beautiful black, white, and orange bird, a Venezuelan troupial, loudly singing a three-note song and happily munching on the flowers of a mesquite tree. Yet, this tree, like most of the native vegetation, was covered with thorns.

On the third day, we moved to the north end of the
island into a beautiful house with wraparound decks and a
kitchen big enough to host a ball in. We were joined there by
David's family, bringing our total number to eight. Our house
had panoramic views of the sea and the desert landscape as
well as an old lighthouse that was very picturesque though
no longer functional.

Each morning, I saw many birds, white-tipped doves,
tropical mockingbirds, and troupials, perched on the top of
straight Yatu cacti, using these tall plants as lookout posts.

Like the troupial in the mesquite, these birds seemed
impervious to the plants' spikes. Did their reptilian skin
shield them from the sharp thorns or were they specially
adapted in some other way to spiky vegetation? Could
Massachusetts birds fare as well?

There were plenty of coconut palms on the island, although they could not survive without human care. Indeed, when we were in the national park, we visited an old, abandoned coconut plantation but saw only one surviving palm tree. Nevertheless, I picked up a small coconut that fell in our yard and sketched it in my hand:

I also sketched a century plant that was probably a few years old since its central spike was not very tall. These plants live about 10 to 30 years, finally boast a tall, central stalk with flowers, and then die. This seems very sad to me, for the plant never gets to see or love its offspring.

In *The Voyage of the Beagle*, Darwin wrote about *Opuntia*, the prickly pear cactus: "I found here a species of cactus, described by Professor Henslow, under the name of *Opuntia darwinii* . . . which was remarkable for the irritability of the stamens, when I inserted either a piece of stick or the end of my finger in the flower. The segments of the perianth also closed on the pistil, but more slowly than the stamens." So, I tried sticking my finger into a lot of prickly pear flowers but never got them to close on me. Perhaps, the prickly pear cactus that was on the island was a different species than the ones Darwin described or perhaps their flowers and anthers were not fully mature.

The best part of the trip was all the time we spent in the national park, which afforded beautiful hiking trails and dramatic rock formations and seascapes. One day when we were driving ever so slowly and carefully down a rutted road and laughing at our situation, I spied out of the corner of my eye a prickly pear cactus in bloom—one single, bright yellow flower amid a sea of pale green cacti—and, suddenly, I felt a great burst of happiness. I think these moments happen when our senses are at their sharpest and we feel most alive.

Happy 2015, Oliver, and I hope you have those happy bursts often in the coming year.

Love,
Sue

Love and Work

OLIVER SACKS, M.D.

2 HORATIO ST. #3G · NEW YORK, NY · 10014
TEL: 212.633.8373 · FAX: 212.633.8928
MAIL@OLIVERSACKS.COM

5.ii.15 [Feb. 5, 2015]

Dear Sue,

I have sad news. It was discovered last month that I have
metastases in the liver from my ocular (uveal) melanoma.
These things rarely metastasize, and I am very glad I had
nine good (and productive) years before the Beast spread.
Uveal mets are not too treatable, tho' there are some
treatments which may <u>retard</u> their spread—for a while,
perhaps, extending "survival" from 6–9 months to 15–16
months. This would be fine if they are <u>good</u> months, months
in which I can write (I have several partly/largely written
books), see friends, travel (a little), enjoy life (even be a bit
silly etc)—months too in which I can "adjust," say "farewell"
to so many and so much I love, and achieve some sense of
"completing" my life and of equanimity in facing this sudden
"Time's Up." I think of the wonderful short autobiography
(entitled <u>My Own Life</u>) which Hume wrote within a single
day (in 1775), when he realized that he was mortally ill.

I am very glad indeed that I finished my autobiography
before this hit me, and the publisher has been very
understanding, advancing its publication date from September
to May 1. I will be getting some "advance reading copies"
(basically the uncorrected ms, without photos, index etc) very
soon, and will enclose one with this letter, or send it on.

<u>You</u> have become an important (and loved) friend (and
mentor) since we met, and I hope to see (lots of) you in the
coming months.

This letter was written on February 5, 2015, but not postmarked
until February 24. When, in January, Oliver become aware of his
terminal illness, he decided to draft letters to friends and family and
mail them all out simultaneously. He also sent an op-ed, titled "My
Own Life," about his condition to *The New York Times* and assumed
it would take a week or two to be published. However, the *Times*
wanted to publish his essay immediately. Since Oliver didn't want his
friends and family to find out about his terminal illness through the
newspaper, Kate sent a group email about his diagnosis on February
18, a day before the op-ed appeared. So, by the time I received this
letter, I was already aware of Oliver's news. I was grief-stricken and
had to reply. But what do you write to someone who knows his days
are soon numbered? In "My Own Life," Oliver wrote that he would
continue to work and have some fun, too, so I struggled to write a
letter that was not too melancholy but still acknowledged the sad
news. I hope I hit the right tone.

February 23, 2015

Dear Oliver,

I've been thinking about books, readers, and writers, and what makes a book endure. Often I'll pick up a book that I once enjoyed and decide to read it a second time, only to find it less gripping. This never happens, however, with your writing. Your books seem as fresh to me with subsequent readings as with the first. Right before we went to Aruba, for example, I decided to read some books about journeys and islands, so I re-read some of Darwin's *The Voyage of the Beagle*, and your *The Island of the Colorblind*. I enjoyed your book just as much with this reading as with earlier ones.

I think this freshness comes in part from the rhythm and flow of your prose. As with your writing, one can read a poem or listen to a song over and over again. Sure—if you listen to a song 100 times a day, you'll get sick of it. But, with some moderation, the song will continue to stimulate and may often provide something new.

When your op-ed came out in *The New York Times*, my brother sent me a very loving email: "You may be losing fathers," he wrote, "but for what it is worth you still have a half-decent brother to rely on." Like a father, you have given me a name, helped me shape a new identity, and have provided guidance, encouragement, inspiration, and love.

. . .

On a lighter note, I am enjoying this rough winter. I recently read a book (which I *will* enjoy with a second reading) called *The Story of Earth* by Robert Hazen. His description of the early earth (volcanoes, violent explosions, asteroid impacts, etc.) put our latest snowstorms and subzero temperatures in perspective. When out walking, I love the way the snow low-pass filters the landscape, rounding out all the sharp edges. When the sun's angle is just right, snow crystals sparkle in very bright colors—colors that change as I change my viewing angle or distance.

After a wild bear feasted off of our birdfeeder last summer, I removed the feeder on a pole and suction-cupped new birdfeeders high up on the windows. It took about three weeks before the first bird, a house finch, visited the feeder. "Brave soul," I thought initially but had to temper my admiration when I saw the finch peck at other birds who, following his example, attempted to come to the feeder. Finally, a junco put his foot down and pecked back, and the finch learned to share.

Most touching is a male cardinal who, despite his flamboyant, ridiculous-looking red pompadour, is quite humble and shy. He watches his mate faithfully when she comes to the feeder just as, this past summer, he worried over his four clumsy children when they first learned to fly. I spy on all this drama with binoculars while reclining on my living room sofa, where I have an unimpeded view of my study window and the feeders attached to it—surely a most decadent way to birdwatch.

For the holidays, Dan gave me an indoor hydroponic garden, which is successfully producing lots of fresh herbs. Of all the plants, cilantro grows best, so I've embarked on a new experiment. Unlike many people, I find cilantro to be repulsive, tasting like soap, yet, when I ask cilantro lovers how the herb tastes to them, they cannot describe the experience. My aversion may be genetic, but, perhaps, I still have a latent ability to appreciate the qualia of cilantro. So, each morning, I eat a few sprigs, and the herb no longer tastes repulsive, though it doesn't taste good. No loss, however. I'm also feeding a wild rabbit who lives under the forsythia bush in our front yard. I leave vegetables and herbs out for her daily and have observed that she rejects bland foods (Romaine lettuce and cucumbers), preferring instead the stronger tasting plants. Indeed, she has a particular yen for cilantro.

All my love,

Stereo Sue

A month later, I sent him more sketches.

march 30, 2015

Dear Oliver,
    Last week, my family and I visited the Dominican Republic, and I drew for you 2 pictures, one of a fern:

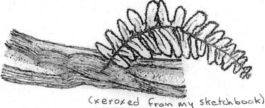

(xeroxed from my sketchbook)

and the other of a cycad leaf:

(xeroxed from my sketchbook)

The cycad was planted, but the fern, an epiphyte, was wild and growing on a palm. I hope these would stir your paleo/mesozoic soul.
    All love, Stereo Sue

On May 19, 2015, I visited Oliver at his home apartment. Although he had recently weathered a gruesome procedure that temporarily starved the tumors in his liver, he looked remarkably good and was writing in high gear. His dining table was covered with books, articles, and yellow legal pads filled with his handwriting. Among other subjects, he was writing about the perceptions of astronauts when floating in space and was interested in Dan's experiences.

I brought Oliver two books to read for fun and an accompanying note. The note was typed, as were all my letters, in 18-point Garamond font; nevertheless, Oliver picked up a large magnifying glass, the size of a CD, to read it.

Dear Oliver,

I don't like coming empty-handed for a visit, so I've brought you two books.

On the one hand, this may be a bad idea because

1. You may have already read the books or know most of what's in them.

2. The print is small.

3. You don't want to be distracted from your writing.

On the other hand, if you want to take a long view, *The Story of Earth* is the book for you. I loved how the author explained the origin of elements, molecules, and rocks, described the violent goings-on in the mantle below us, and discussed the tantalizing possibility that life is responsible for the vast diversity of minerals on earth.

As a cryptogamicophile,* you may look askance at the

---

* I made up the word "cryptogamicophile." Cryptogamous plants, such as ferns, are those that reproduce through spores, not seeds, and these were Oliver's favorite plants. So a cryptogamicophile was a fern lover.

title of the second book, *The Triumph of Seeds*, but I enjoyed learning (among other things) about a new, surprising view of the Carboniferous forest, the many connections between seeds and human culture, and the co-evolution of nuts and rodent teeth!

Oliver showed me the book he was currently reading—a huge tome about Pavlov. Since he liked to read by lying on his back and holding the book aloft, he had cut some books into parts with each part held together by binder clips.

As we drank green tea, I told Oliver that I was going to retire from teaching at the end of the year. He looked shocked. Love and work, Oliver had written (paraphrasing Freud) were the two most important things in life. Writing was a significant part of Oliver's work. In the ten years that I had known him, despite one medical insult after another, he had written four substantial books. When we first began corresponding, Oliver typed out his letters with two fingers on an IBM Selectric typewriter. When this became too difficult, he wrote by hand. And in the last weeks of his life, he would dictate his letters. He never stopped working and writing. So, I hastily added that I was retiring, not to put my feet up, but to write more. Indeed, I never forgot Oliver's stunned look, and it motivated me to complete my second book, *Coming to Our Senses: A Boy Who Learned to See, A Girl Who Learned to Hear, and How We All Discover the World*.

When it was time for a goodbye hug, I strode over to Oliver with my arms spread wide and said, very loudly (for Oliver heard poorly), "I love you." I assumed he knew that, but I wanted to say it out loud, not knowing whether we would ever see each other again.

OLIVER SACKS, M.D.

2 HORATIO ST. #3G · NEW YORK, NY · 10014
TEL: 212.633.8373 · FAX: 212.633.8928
MAIL@OLIVERSACKS.COM   6/6/15

Dear Sue

You are (over!) loading me with books—all of them good.
I am in the middle of <u>The Story of Earth</u>, and loving how
Hazen brings together Chemistry, Geology, Petrology,
Mineralogy—with life, which we can (begin to) do now, in a
way unimaginable even 20 years ago.

. . .

I have been entertained by Dan's description of his
sensation (and thoughts and feelings) in space—and will (if
he permits) incorporate some of them in a little piece about
(being in) space I am writing.

He must be very pre-occupied now by the coming Robot
Festival (show, competition, game, whatever), and deep into
the 28 May issue of <u>Nature</u> (which is making me think of
"A.I.," of Grey Walter's "tortoises" (which I saw as a
schoolboy in 1948), and the amazing ways forward,
conceptually, and technically, of the last 20 years. A grand
subject—and one which goes with the exploration of space.

love,

Olly

Lead Birthday

May 2015 was not the last time I saw Oliver. On July 9, 2015, Oliver turned eighty-two, and as was his custom, he hosted a birthday party in his apartment. Although he knew and we knew that this would be Oliver's last birthday, he did not want sympathy or talk of death. He and Kate provided the usual fare, smoked salmon and sushi, and soon his twenty-five guests were eating and engaged in multiple conversations.

Oliver and I talked about the very subject upon which our friendship began: vision. He took me to a small room off his living room to show me a fossil of an extinct arthropod, a trilobite. These fossils, which are about 540 million years old, are the first fossils that convincingly reveal an animal with image-forming eyes. Although Oliver was to die seven weeks later, he was still thinking about what he would write next, and he was stimulated by the many ways that different animals see. Sea urchins, he excitedly pointed out, have light-sensitive cells on their many tube feet. What, he wondered, would it be like to see as a sea urchin? He had watched an octopus once and felt that the octopus, a highly intelligent creature, was studying him with the same concentration with which he was watching the octopus. He felt a kinship with the octopus and with lemurs, too, whose large front-facing eyes are similar to ours. Indeed, he was going to North Carolina the next week to see the lemur colony there. Shortly after this conversation, as it was getting late and Oliver was talking with others, Dan and I quietly departed. Oliver would not have wanted a tearful good-bye.

All these remarks got me thinking about my own experience watching animals. Could I observe them closely enough to read their minds? Two days later, I sent Oliver this letter.

July 11, 2015

Dear Oliver,

Dan and I really enjoyed your birthday party. . . . Thanks so much for the invitation.

I was struck by your discussion of vision in other animals and your description of watching an octopus watching you. This reminded me of a singular encounter I had with a frog several years back while teaching my students about gaze stabilization in people and other animals. I had the students observe the vestibulo-ocular reflex and (by spinning a large, vertically striped umbrella) optokinetic nystagmus in each other.[*] Then, we watched a crayfish in an optokinetic drum perform optokinetic movements with its stalked eyes. Although the crayfish behaved, in this sense, like us, I didn't feel any particular kinship with the crawdad. But then I picked up a frog, a common leopard frog (*Rana pipiens*), and our eyes met and locked. What I saw in the frog's eyes was fear, and I saw this as clearly as I would see fear in the eyes of a member of my

---

[*] The vestibulo-ocular reflex generates eye movements that stabilize our gaze while our head is moving, whereas optokinetic nystagmus generates eye movements that allow us to track moving objects while our head is stationary.

own species. "Don't worry, little guy," I said to the frog, "I'm not going to hurt you. I'm going to put you on a platform and tilt your whole body in one direction to show how you respond by tilting your head in the opposite way." This, the frog did admirably, but it was our intimate visual exchange that has stayed with me and made me feel closer to frogs ever since.

There was another incident that happened that day with the very same frog. At the end of class, I put the frog in a dish, covering the dish with my hand, to take him back to his aquarium, located two floors below. This was clearly a bad idea because, when I got to the second-floor stair landing, my hand slipped and the frog exploded out of the dish, sailing down the open stairwell. "Watch out!" I yelled to an unsuspecting student on the ground floor, "Falling frog!" Then I closed my eyes because I didn't want to see the consequences of frog meeting floor. But, when I opened my eyes, the frog was hopping about. Indeed, it took me and the half-traumatized student quite some time to catch the frog and return him to his aquarium. For the next two weeks, I checked on him every day, concerned that he was suffering internal injuries. But the frog seemed fine. His wide body and small mass must have permitted a soft landing.

I think the book by Nilsson you are going to read is *Animal Eyes* by both Land and Nilsson. That book helped me understand what seemed like a bizarre behavior in pigeons— the way they bob their heads while foraging. It turns out that this is a common behavior in several species of ground-feeding birds. When they walk, they first thrust their head forward and then keep it still while the rest of the body catches up. Their gaze remains stable while the head is still so they won't miss seeing any tasty morsels that might be present by their side.

I hope you have fun or had fun with the lemurs, our frontal-eyed cousins. Eye-movement studies reveal that macaques have faster eye movements than people. Lemurs, too, could be eye movement superstars!

Love,

Stereo Sue

Saying Goodbye

Oliver had mentioned to me at his birthday party that he would have to go back to the hospital after his trip to see the lemurs. The news sounded ominous. On August 9, I drew and sent a card with his favorite animals.

9 AUGUST, 2015

DEAR OLIVER,

THINKING OF YOU.

LOVE,
Stereo Sue

For the rest of the summer, Oliver remained very much on my mind. As I went about my day, I kept trying to find events, usually involving animals, which I could write to Oliver about. In my next, and what turned out to be last, letter, I sketched and described an encounter between geese and a fox.

Aug. 18, 2015

Dear Oliver,

Yesterday, as I was biking toward the lake on Mount Holyoke's campus, I spied a red fox approaching the water. He was young and lean with a glossy coat. When he got to the water's edge, five geese swam up, forming a line, directly opposite the fox on the shore.

I got off my bike to watch. Although these geese have young ones, the goslings were nowhere in sight. What followed was a staring contest between the fox and the geese. After some time, the fox turned around and walked off into the high grass. His step was jaunty, as if to hide the fact that he had just been bested by five birds. Meanwhile, the geese broke formation, turned around, and swam away with their heads high.

Four of the birds were Canadian geese, but the fifth was a white goose. While the Canadian geese come and go, the white goose lives permanently at the lake. Named Jorge by the students, he's become a campus mascot with his own Facebook page. Jorge joins whatever flock of geese or ducks comes to the lake, but he stays put when the others fly away. (Does he ever pine for a mate of his own?) Yesterday, the Canadian geese were defending their young, and Jorge stood (swam) in solidarity with them. "Way to go, Jorge!" I shouted as I got back on my bike. Jorge turned in my direction though the other geese did not. This is not the first time that Jorge has responded to my calls. I think he knows his name.

Sending all good thoughts and wishes your way.

All my love,
Stereo Sue

I realized sometime later that I must have identified Oliver with Jorge the goose. They were both "odd ducks" (so to speak), but they fought fiercely for those most vulnerable.

Oliver wrote his last letter to me only three weeks before he died. Although he was failing quickly, with the help of Kate, office assistant Hallie Parker, and his lover Billy Hayes, he was still sending letters to his friends. Since 2010, he had written all of his letters to me by hand, but now, too weak to write, he dictated this last one.

Oliver began this letter with the salutation "Dearest Sue," not "Dear Sue," recalling for me a conversation I had with him in December 2009. He told me then that he was bothered by the salutation "Dear" at the beginning of letters. "Dear," he felt should be reserved for someone you hold dear as opposed to a general salutation used even with strangers. So, when he began this letter with "Dearest Sue," I knew this letter would be heartfelt. It was actually composed nine days before my letter about Jorge, but I want Oliver, who died on August 30, 2015, to have the last word.

 OLIVER SACKS, M.D.

2 HORATIO ST. #3G · NEW YORK, NY · 10014   August 9, 2015
TEL: 212.633.8373 · FAX: 212.633.8928
MAIL@OLIVERSACKS.COM

Dearest Sue,

When I got your first letter, with excerpts of your journal, in 2004, I had, we had, no idea that a rich friendship would blossom out of our initial contact, one which extends, of course, to include Dan as well. I was particularly glad to see you both at my birthday party last month.

I'm afraid I've gone rapidly downhill in this last month. I am very weak and lose a liter or more of "ascites" daily, which we drain off morning and evening. I have, however, no major discomforts and, with the enormous and devoted support of Kate and Billy, keep as active as I can, and writing as much as I can, though I do not know whether I will be able to finish some of the many projects I started, including the one on floating in space. I am too ill at this point to receive visitors or phone calls, but your letters (with their marvelous little drawings) are always fun to receive.

This is not quite farewell, but it is getting close to it, for I doubt I will last out this month.

A deep and stimulating friendship with you has been a wonderful and unexpected addition to my life in these last ten years, and I am exceedingly grateful for this.

With all my love,

Text and Image Credits

Photo Insert

Photo 1: copyright © 1993 Magic Eye Inc.

Photo 2: copyright © Karen Crawford

Photo 3: copyright © Andrew J. Barry and Susan R. Barry

Photo 4: from Bela Julesz, *Foundations of Cyclopean Perception*,
foreword by Thomas V. Papathomas, fig. 2.4-1, copyright © 2006
Massachusetts Institute of Technology, by permission of The
MIT Press.

Photo 5: copyright © Malcolm Feinstein

Photos 6 and 7 by Ralph M. Siegel

Photo 9: copyright © Dan Barry

Acknowledgments

This book is an ode to friendship, letter-writing, and Oliver Sacks. I thank Oliver for his kindness and warmth, for listening, for giving me confidence and a voice, and for sharing his thoughts. Never again will my walk to the mailbox be filled with the same sense of anticipation as when I expected a letter from Horatio Street with the picture of a handsome squid by the return address.

I owe a great debt to Kate Edgar, Oliver's longtime editor, for her friendship, support, and wise advice. When Oliver first came to my house, I asked him about Kate and he responded, "She has very good judgment." Thanks, too, to Oliver's office assistants, Hailey Wojcik and Hallie Parker. I am very grateful to The Oliver Sacks Foundation for permission to publish Oliver's letters to me.

I thank Rosalie Winard, whom I met through Oliver, for her friendship, photographs, and insights, and for arranging many happy visits with Oliver and Kate.

I must not forget to thank the US Postal Service for reliably and efficiently ferrying Oliver's and my letters between New York and Massachusetts.

I thank my optometrist, Theresa Ruggiero, for guiding me though vision therapy and the revelatory experiences of first seeing in 3D.

Along with Theresa, optometrists Paul Harris and Leonard Press helped me prepare some of my letters to Oliver concerning the critical period and recovery of stereovision. I thank Robert Krulwich of National Public Radio for his *Morning Edition* program about me called "Going Binocular: Susan's First Snowfall," and Dempsey Rice for her videos, posted on YouTube, of me and Oliver.

For their friendship and encouragement during my letter-writing years, I thank Cynthia Beauregard, Carol Chiodi, Alan Copsey, Kate Edgar, Barbara Ehrlich, Daniel Feinstein, Deborah Feinstein, Janice Grzesinski, Kathleen Jackson, Elizabeth Korn, Priscilla Mandrachia, Claire Schub, Elizabeth Sokolow, Rose Ann Wasserman, Lawrence Weschler, and Rosalie Winard, as well as my Mount Holyoke colleagues, Rachel Fink, Linda Laderach, Andy Lass, John Lemly, Chris Pyle, Bill Quillian, Stan Rachootin, Margaret Robinson, and Diana Stein. Special thanks to Alan Copsey, Kate Edgar, Daniel Feinstein, and Rachel Fink for reading an earlier draft of this book. Any errors that remain are my own.

I thank my invaluable book agent, Lisa Adams of The Garamond Agency, for guiding me through the book proposal and the whole book publishing business as she did for my two previous books.

I thank Andy Barry for the cycad anaglyph, Rosalie Winard for photos of me and Oliver, Dan Barry for the compass hat photo (and compass hat!), Karen Crawford for the beautiful photo of a squid embryo, Tom Baccei and Cheri Smith for the stereogram in the Magic Eye book, Lina Granada for help with the Feiffer illustration, and the late Ralph M. Siegel and his wife, Jasmine Siegel, for photos taken during Oliver's trip to my home.

I am very grateful to Matthew Lore and Batya Rosenblum at The Experiment for seeing the promise in this book and to Batya for her careful edits, encouraging me always to keep the reader in mind. Thanks, too, to managing editor Zach Pace, Juliann Barbato for thoughtful copy editing, Ann J. Kirschner for proofreading, and Beth Bugler for the jacket design and interior book design.

As always, I thank my family: my children Jenny and Andy Barry, their spouses David German and Katya Kosheleva, my granddaughter, Jessie, and the granddaughter about to be born. Above all, I thank my swashbuckling husband, Dan Barry, for encouraging me to take risks when I wavered. It is to Dan for a half century of fun, love, and support that I dedicate this book.

About the Author

Susan R. Barry is professor emeritus of biological sciences and neuroscience at Mount Holyoke College and the author of two previous books, *Fixing My Gaze: A Scientist's Journey Into Seeing in Three Dimensions* and *Coming to Our Senses: A Boy Who Learned to See, A Girl Who Learned to Hear, and How We All Discover the World.* She lives with her husband in Massachusetts.

stereosue.com